Evaluating Major Components of Two-Year Colleges

Richard I. Miller, Editor

College and University Personnel Association

Contents

Figures

Preface

The purpose of this book is to assist administrators in two-year colleges understand and initiate better policies and procedures for evaluating students, full-time and part-time faculty members, administrators, programs, student services, external relations, and the institutions themselves. Written by practicing community college administrators and faculty members, it combines theory, research, and exemplary practices in a meaningful, sound, and understandable manner. This book may be unique in that it focuses on how to evaluate almost all major components of two-year colleges.

Much literature on evaluation has been developed for four-year colleges and universities since the early 1970s as a reaction to financial austerity and to calls for greater accountability and better management. The two-year sector, however, has lagged far behind in adding significant and substantial research and materials to this national dialogue. It is encouraging to note a significant rise in these interests in recent years and the next decade should see a continuing growth in this knowledge base for two-year colleges.

The book is written primarily for busy administrators who are interested in evaluation and can find time to read syntheses of research as well as successful practices but who do not have time to study and digest the growing number of serious research studies that are related to major dimensions of evaluation. In addition, busy Board members should find

the book of considerable interest because it relates to evaluation, which
will be one of the most important community college issues of the 1990s,
and one which already is on almost every Board meeting agenda. The
book also should be useful for faculty committees in two-year colleges
who are working on evaluation issues that relate to one or more of the
chapters. Individual faculty members should be able to know and better
understand dimensions of evaluation that are of interest to them.

Chapter one considers the role of evaluation in two-year colleges—
discussing societal influences such as the public's demand for accountability, definitions of accountability, and types of evaluation. Implications of evaluation are analyzed.

Chapter two focuses on evaluating student performance. Beginning
with purposes, it discusses various approaches. Evaluating the effectiveness of general education as an aspect of student learning, and
terminal or final evaluative processes are considered. Value-added evaluation includes the Florida and Georgia approach. Some characteristics
of effective student performance assessment are presented.

Chapter three discusses evaluating full-time faculty members, considering what and why we are evaluating, validity, self-evaluation, student evaluations of teaching, colleague evaluation, growth contracts, and
appeal and grievance procedures.

Evaluating part-time faculty members receives attention in chapter
four. Reasons for, as well as some concerns about, using part-timers are
given. The evaluation should judge content expertise, instructional design skills, and delivery skills. A comprehensive evaluation model is
included.

Evaluating academic program effectiveness in chapter five considers
common myths, such as the belief that an institution does not need a
program review process if programs have been accredited by national
or regional bodies, and the myth that there is only one way to conduct
a program review. Issues in program evaluation, models, and criteria
for program evaluation also are discussed.

Chapter six on evaluating student services programs considers the
why, what, how, who, and when dimensions. Characteristics of a good
model for student services programs are offered.

Evaluating administrative performance is the topic of chapter seven,
and it begins with a rationale for administrative evaluation. Planning,
appraisal methods, and difficulties and concerns related to administrative evaluation are analyzed.

Chapter eight considers the evaluation of external relations, including
state and local government, business and industry, and community ser-

vices. Ways of evaluating institutional effectiveness for various external clientele are outlined.

Evaluating institutional effectiveness is the focus of chapter nine. Purposes, problems, and characteristics of successful institutional evaluation systems are considered, and a comprehensive model for institutional evaluation is presented.

Chapter ten concludes with the future roles of evaluation in two-year colleges. Economic and demographic issues form a backdrop for increasing future needs for retraining programs. Concerns about the aging of the American professoriate are discussed. The future will bring pressures for greater accountability, better service to economically deprived students, and educating the whole person.

Chapter authors as well as the editor want to express sincere appreciation to family members and close friends who facilitated our work through their moral support and encouragement.

Melissa Brown was very helpful in editing the manuscript as well as in cross-checking the references. Hope Socci contributed her considerable skills and cooperation in typing and checking the manuscript.

Finally, we acknowledge the unknown audience that is "out there." Researching and writing are twin lonelinesses that afflict all writers. It is the hope for silent communication of ideas with countless others that carries its own reward. This touch of missionary zeal and a strong sense of service remain stronger in two-year colleges than in other sectors of postsecondary education.

Richard I. Miller

Contributors

Corrine M. Brown is Director, Management Information Systems, at Hocking Technical College, Nelsonville, Ohio.

Judith Bush is Director, Adult Learning Services, Ohio University-Belmont, St. Clairsville, Ohio.

Robert L. Cherry is Director of Records, and the Minority Task Force, Clark Technical College, Springfield, Ohio.

Barbara Come is a Reading Specialist, Scioto County Schools, Portsmouth, Ohio.

Charles E. Finley is an Instructor, Graphics Communications, Columbus State Community College, Columbus, Ohio.

Peter H. Grant is Director of Admissions at North Central Technical College, Mansfield, Ohio.

Dwight Greer is Assistant Director of Student Services at Ohio University-Zanesville, Zanesville, Ohio.

Priscilla Haag-Mutter is a Career Development Specialist at the Career Center of Sinclair Community College, Dayton, Ohio.

J. Dennis Hart is Director of Business Technologies at Marion Technical College, Marion, Ohio.

Mary-Louise Holloway is Chairperson, Nursing Technology, at Columbus State Community College, Columbus, Ohio.

Edward W. Holzapfel, Jr. is Dean of Administrative Services at Washington Technical College, Marietta, Ohio.

C. Wayne Jones is Dean of Administrative Services at Southern State Community College, Hillsboro, Ohio.

Michael G. Kaiser is Director of Public Relations and Advertising at Ohio University-Belmont, St. Clairsville, Ohio.

Katherine D. Kalinos is Assistant Professor, Medical Laboratory Technology, Clark Technical College, Springfield, Ohio.

Deborah Jean Kladivko is Director of Student Services at Ohio University-Zanesville, Zanesville, Ohio.

Sanford A. Lane is Dean of Technologies at Rio Grande College and Community College, Rio Grande, Ohio.

Stephen J. Midkiff is Counselor/Director of Records at Shawnee State University, Portsmouth, Ohio.

Lynn M. Rector is Director of Student Life, Clark Technical College, Springfield, Ohio.

Stephen Rostek is Assistant Academic Dean at Muskingum Area Technical College, Zanesville, Ohio.

Gene Wilson is Director of Financial Aid at Shawnee State University, Portsmouth, Ohio.

Editor

Professor Richard I. Miller teaches and advises graduate students in higher education and coordinates the Educational Leadership Area Program at Ohio University. Other classroom teaching experiences include the University of Illinois at Urbana, the University of Kentucky, Southwest Texas State University, and Cornell University as a visiting scholar.

Senior academic administrative experiences include academic vice-presidencies at Southwest Texas State University, the State University of New York at Brockport, and Baldwin-Wallace College. Other administrative experiences include serving as a senior academic program officer with the Illinois Board of Higher Education; executive secretary for a national committee appointed by President Johnson on experimentation and innovation in the public schools; and director of a program on educational change at the University of Kentucky. He initiated in 1986 and co-chairs a three-year study of the National Committee for the Enhancement of Institutional Research in Two-Year Colleges.

His writings include four Jossey-Bass books and a booklet: *Evaluating Faculty for Promotion and Tenure* (1987), *Institutional Assessment for Self-Improvement* (1981), *The Assessment of College Performance* (1979), *Developing Programs for Faculty Evaluation* (1974), *Evaluating Faculty Performance* (1972); seven other books; a dozen chapters in books; several dozen articles; and several research projects. Dr. Miller is co-editor of *Issues in*

Personnel Management, a 1988 publication in the Jossey-Bass series on New Directions for Community Colleges.

Consultation, speaking and workshop experiences include well over 100 campuses in every section of the nation and numerous international assignments. Dr. Miller has served in positions of responsibility in several national associations, and he has received several awards and honors.

1

The Role of Evaluation in Two-Year Colleges

By Judith Bush and Michael Kaiser

E valuation is recognized as an important part of education in general, but its role in the two-year college environment has received less attention.

Evaluation as a process and as a product is not new to institutional thought. As early as 4000 years B.C. in China, government officials set up a system for the hiring and assessment of civil servants; and the early Greeks and Romans and the universities of medieval Europe had established ways to evaluate teaching. Even in this early period students were often involved in the evaluation process through hiring and firing teachers (Hofstadter and Metzger 1969). Evaluation of an informal nature has no doubt always been a part of higher education. It is impossible to imagine a time in which students did not discuss the relative merits of faculty members, administrators or institutions.

Societal Influences

Higher education was affected by three events in recent decades—two were based on increased funding support from all governmental levels, and the third was the outgrowth of student unrest during the Vietnam era. The first influx of funds came as a result of what is commonly called the "Sputnik phenomenon." In the late 1950s and

1960s funding from mainly federal sources brought about an increased emphasis on the sciences and mathematics. Higher education was impacted most directly by massive reviews and revisions of curricula. With this increase in funding, the government felt the need to justify these great expenditures; therefore, government agencies and educators felt that it was necessary to devise formal evaluation processes.

The second occurrence came in the 1960s and early 1970s when the federal and state governments once again funnelled money into higher education to support social action programs as part of the War on Poverty. These anti-poverty programs were an effort to bring educationally neglected people into the mainstream of American life. Once again the increase in federal spending brought about the need to justify the expenditures, and formal evaluation received a further push.

The student unrest of the Vietnam era impacted higher education in many ways, including the installation of new evaluation processes, especially faculty evaluation. The focus then switched from the evaluation of faculty to other areas of higher education.

> The current heightened interest in collegiate evaluation started with faculty evaluation in the mid sixties, spurred by student protests on some campuses. In the 1970s administrative evaluation came on the scene, and it too has developed rapidly. One should not be surprised, therefore, to find new interest in assessing programs, departments, and institutions. In other words, all aspects of colleges and universities are being increasingly evaluated (Miller 1979, p.x).

The 1980s have opened a Pandora's box of areas in higher education requiring formal and informal evaluation, and the two-year campus has not escaped this trend. The recent emphasis on excellence and access has made evaluation a more essential aspect in general planning than at any previous time.

The public demand for accountability also has accentuated the recent focus on excellence in higher education. Although no clear cut definition exists as to what "excellence" is, every institution strives for improvement.

> Obviously all want to achieve high quality instruction. No institution is on record as having selected mediocrity or less as a goal. And presumably all want excellence especially in educational programs. After all, two-year colleges exist as corporate institutions principally to provide instruction according to their prescribed missions as best they can, always striving for improvement. By not

really knowing what truly constitutes excellence colleges tend to select those measures that best demonstrate this quality for them and may tend to ignore those that do not (McCleod and Carter 1986, p. 15).

The role of evaluation is to assess worth and improve the processes that enhance quality. Palmer (1983) noted that society often inappropriately applies evaluation criteria for four-year institutions to judge excellence in the community college setting.

Access—making postsecondary education available to a wider segment of the population—is an urgent need, and two-year institutions have led the way in this effort. Evaluation is being used as a tool to assess demographic changes, market conditions, curriculum developments, technological advances, and educational delivery systems. In general, two-year colleges have found it necessary to evaluate all aspects of their missions more often than four-year institutions.

Evaluation Defined

Evaluation is defined as valuing or assessing the worth of a subject, and it is also described in terms of its purposes. The *Encyclopedia of Educational Research* (Mitzel, ed., 1982) says that evaluation makes a judgment on the worth of the object of the evaluation, aids in the decision-making process, and recognizes the political ramifications.

The major element of functional evaluation is the judgment of worth which is a primary function of decision-makers, such as a college president, a department chairperson, or a member of a Board of Trustees. Making decisions requires the pertinent information which then is organized in terms of how effectively the activity meets its goals. That is, how well does a teacher do his/her job; how well does a program meet the needs of the community; how well does a physical plant function; or how well does technology enhance the delivery of education?

Gathering information on the subject to be evaluated is the function of the "reporter" who provides the decision-maker with the information necessary to determine the worth of the activity. The reporter makes no decisions about value or worth, although internal and external forces may attempt to influence the data passed on to the decision-maker.

Decision-makers must also take into account internal and external political influences and ramifications of the evaluation process; such as "the greatest good for the greatest number," cost effectiveness, and special interest lobbies. For example, if a departmental chairperson lowered program entrance requirements in order to revitalize lagging enrollments, the political pressure he would exert on a decision-maker would be internal. On the other hand, if a state senator wanted the enrollment in the same department to increase in order to make good a promise to expand the delivery of a technology to the local area, this pressure on the decision-maker would be an external political force.

Types of Evaluation

Evaluation can be either informal or formal. Informal evaluation does not have structure and may not have clearly defined goals. It is initiated internally or externally and it may or may not be politically motivated. An information evaluation could be as simple as one student telling another that "X" institution is a good or bad place to attend. The student has based his or her evaluation on intuition, second-hand information, or experience—in other words, on fact or fiction or a combination of the two. Informal evaluations can have a significant impact on institutions; they may be the most common form of evaluation in postsecondary education.

Formal evaluation requires a definite structure, goals, procedures, allocation of resources and time; it can be either internal or external, or politically or not politically motivated. The accreditation process is a prominent example of formal evaluation. The self-study phase of accreditation is internal while site visit by the accreditation team in the next phase is external.

Often there is an over-lap of formal and informal evaluation. For example, even in the formalized accreditation process, informal evaluation is accepted as input from the community. Once the type of evaluation that is needed is determined, a method—or more often a combination of methods—is investigated.

Methodology

In choosing a method of evaluation, two decisions need to be considered: First, is the evaluation to be formative or summative, and then, is it to be qualitative or quantitative? Scriven (1966) distinguishes between formative and summative by the timing of the evaluation and how the results of the evaluation are used. He defines formative evaluation as a continuing process during the activity characterized by immediate and frequent feedback with the general aim of improvement. He defines summative evaluation as that which takes place after the activity has been completed with the criteria of success and/or outcomes examined at that time. In both cases, Scriven states that evaluation is the assessment of merit.

The next decision concerns whether the evaluation should be primarily quantitative or qualitative. Since research is the systematic gathering of data to explain events, the reporter or the decision-maker needs to determine whether to use quantitative or qualitative tools. The quantitative approach converts evaluation data into statistics from which decisions can be made. The qualitative approach deals with values, emotions, and other less measurable data. Most reporters will employ a combination of both of these tools for presentation of their analyses to the decision-maker. Some aspects of one method may apply better to one situation than to another, and the key to successful methodology is to be flexible enough to apply different methodologies to fit different needs (Churchman 1980). After the data is collected, organized, analyzed, and prioritized, it becomes the decision-maker's responsibility to review the alternatives, realize the political implications, and arrive at a conclusion. Churchman sees the primary purpose of evaluation as an aid to educational decision-making.

A Simple Model of Evaluation

Decision-makers should be able to conceptualize evaluation in order to understand better what takes place during the process. It may be helpful to make a graphic representation of the idea to be analyzed. Evaluation models are seldom static because of the constantly changing environment in which they must function. Strother and Klus (1982) claim that evaluation designs take one of two forms:

> Whether simple or complex, these designs have two things in common: first, they are meaningful only to the extent that they make comparisons possible; and second, they operate within some time constraint. Comparisons are essential whether the evaluation is as simple as a yes or no answer to the question, "Did you find this program helpful?" or as complicated as a longitudinal, double-blend multivariate experimental analysis . . . (p. 134).

What follows is a simple model of the evaluation process (see Figure 1). In any evaluation, input data can be either internal or external or a combination of both. Faculty, students, administration, facilities, budget constraints, and institutional politics are some of the sources of internal

A SIMPLE MODEL OF AN EVALUATION PROCESS

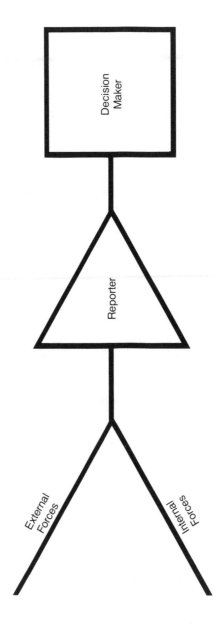

Decision Maker

Reporter

External Forces

Internal Forces

Figure 1

forces which produce data from which decisions are made. Examples of external forces include community, government regulations and legislation, special interest groups, outside funding, and business and industrial demands.

The reporter is the person or persons designated to make the initial analysis of the incoming data and to sort out the essential information to forward to the decision-maker. The reporter functions as a collector, analyzer, and filterer of the data. In theory, the reporter should maintain a neutral and unbiased position, while in practice this is quite difficult. The reporter is often pressured, particularly by special interest groups, to report what might not be purely unbiased data.

The decision-maker has the responsibility of the final determination of worth. In some cases, the decision-maker may do the investigative job of the reporter; however, in an endeavor to maintain neutrality, the reporter and the decision-maker should be two separate functions. This model represents the concept of evaluation in very general terms. In the following chapters, models more specific to areas of concern within the two-year college setting are presented.

Implications of Evaluation

While two-year and four-year colleges have quite different environments, many evaluation principles and practices apply to both of these sectors; however, some differences do exist. The considerable diversity of the two-year college course offerings as well as their student body require more flexible evaluation models. Standardization may be more difficult from this point of view although the more common autocratic governance style of two-year college leaders may make standardization easier. The greater percentage of part-time faculty on two-year campuses means that evaluation is not only necessary to maintain standards, but that it must be done quickly to stay abreast of the rapid turnover that four-year institutions do not experience.

Change usually comes slowly to four-year institutions, while the two-year colleges live in a constantly changing climate. Programs that seem to meet community needs today may require adjustment almost overnight. Two-year institutions have traditionally had to adapt more quickly to pressures from within and from without, and often this rate of change does not allow for formal evaluation. As a result, evaluation may be primarily informal. The consequences of neglecting formal evaluation may be similar to those of neglecting good planning, which may be unforeseen and possibly have negative results (Hammons 1987).

Among the many obstacles to evaluation in the two-year setting are the lack of clear goals, conflict with other objectives, lack of adequate resources, political pressures, and lack of priorities. Strother and Klus (1982) write about the importance of clear goals and objectives:

> A clear statement of objectives, then, is desirable for several reasons. It defines the criteria on which the evaluation of the program will be based. It also forces the programmer to think in terms of the intended accomplishment, thus enhancing the chances for success, and it provides a justification for the activity (p. 125).

However, if the goals and objectives are unrealistic, the chances of a valid evaluation diminish, which is also the case when goals and objectives are not specific enough. Realistic and specific goals are not difficult to achieve if careful planning procedures are carried out early in the evaluation process.

Inadequate resources is a different type of problem, and one that is often more difficult to remedy. A successful evaluation plan needs adequate money, time, and personnel; evaluation plans have failed to achieve satisfactory results because of the deletion of one or more of these resources.

When every perceivable problem or barrier to successful evaluation is assessed, the decision-maker must then carefully consider the priorities. Completing the steps in the evaluation process will work best when the most important goals and objectives are ranked according to the priorities of the decision-maker. Usually these are directly related to the mission and the philosophy of the institution.

Summary

Formal and/or informal evaluation in some form takes place constantly at every institution. Two-year college administrators should be particularly sensitive to this reality and therefore initiate formal evaluation whenever potentially meaningful and feasible. Active formal evaluation strategies can forestall evaluations thrust upon the institution from external sources. Evaluations need to be carefully planned to fit the uniqueness of each institution, to satisfy both school and community needs and demands, and to help the institution to grow in a positive direction. The demands of budget constraints, changing demographics, and the diversity of staff and student populations require creative and possibly even unusual evaluation designs.

Although research in evaluation in two-year colleges is growing, it is still sparse. Researchers can find a challenge in studying and designing appropriate models for different areas of evaluation, and their findings can aid two-year college administrators considerably. Our colleagues have attempted just that, and what follows are the results of their research into specific areas of two-year college evaluation. It is our hope that these chapters will elicit critical responses leading to further understanding of most major facets of evaluation in two-year colleges.

2

Evaluating Student Performance

By Sanford A. Lane and Stephen J. Midkiff

I n the context of current concern for educational accountability, evaluating the performance of college students means measuring the impact of the college experience on the students. The concern for accountability also is now a matter of high interest in state legislatures across the country. Although the four-year colleges and universities have been the primary target of this concern for accountability, the two-year colleges are drawing increasing attention.

All postsecondary institutions are in greater competition for fewer high school graduates in a time of stabilized funding levels. An increasing proportion of students view community colleges as serving primarily their communities, where students can learn skills to provide them with economic and social mobility (Dziech 1986). At the same time, a persistent contingent of students are enrolled because it is a less expensive two years toward a baccalaureate degree. The demands of two-year colleges to prove their worth is imminent.

Academicians also have expressed growing concerns for educational quality, the hallmark of accountability. Although their interest has been largely focused upon the effects on students in baccalaureate programs, there is much applicability to the students of two-year institutions. This chapter will present some of the considerations which appear to be most pertinent to the two-year colleges and which will provide a head start toward evaluating student performance.

11

Purposes

There may be a tendency for some colleges to acknowledge what other colleges are doing in assessing student performance and to enter this arena just to keep up. Time and money can be wasted and goodwill lost if a college does not establish its reasons for an evaluation *first*. The need may be to discover why graduates are not recruited by industries or why they do not pass licensing exams, or the need may be to respond to workplace feedback. Whatever the reasons, they should be identified and be made the objective for direction and focus so that the assessment information is right for the situation (Ewell 1985a). There may be few incentives for faculty or administrators to be interested in or to use student assessment information if the heavy emphasis is on head counts instead of academic quality. But it has also been observed that the concept of assessment is accepted better when faculty and department chairs can have and use the data to examine and improve curricula (Ewell 1985b). A worthwhile performance should be usable and should be placed in the hands of staff at the curricular level.

Approaches

Two fundamental approaches to student performance evaluation have evolved from the current emphasis on accountability: (1) measure what the students *know* after they have received their education (competency), and (2) measure the *change* in knowledge or development that has occurred as a result of having received their education (value-added). The two approaches are not exclusive, but a college's administrators probably will find one of them more suitable to their purpose than the other.

With whatever approach is used, if there is to be evaluation, there likely will be testing. Further testing of students, beyond their curricular examinations, may meet with some resistance from them or they may shun such further attempts at testing (Spangehl 1987). The college probably should anticipate student resistance and plan some attractive reason for participation, perhaps offering incentives for participation such as small inducements in the form of coupons or certificates for restaurants (Moden and Williford 1987).

Testing may seem to be a direct and straightforward means of assessing student learning, and in some instances it will be so, but a suggestion for caution is made by Banta and Fisher (1987):

> A number of [standardized] tests for college students can be readily
> obtained . . . and the results will be available quickly in a form that
> is relatively easy to interpret. However, there is evidence that an
> assessment program based on testing alone is simplistic and incom-
> plete at best . . . Even a cursory review reveals that no single stand-
> ardized test measures more than a fraction of what teachers hope
> their students will learn in a course of study (p. 44).

These authors subsequently imply that aside from a partial lack of
test data on factual learning, the "incomplete" aspect is the fact that
tests will not provide information about *why* students are not achieving
expected results. They propose that student questionnaires and interviews be used to provide supplementary information toward answering
"why?" Such information would be directed toward improving the educational process and would supplement the cognitive information provided by tests. While Banta and Fisher address the testing of four-year
graduates, any kind of terminal testing of two-year graduates may suffer
the same shortcoming and may also benefit from supplementary information.

Another kind of supplementary evaluation is being used by community colleges to study the effectiveness of vocational programs in providing training relevant to particular occupations and industries (Ewell
1984, 27). Competencies to perform certain tasks as a result of college
training are examined through the use of skill demonstrations by the
students and feedback from employers of graduates or former students.

The General Education Component

The literature is extensive about student attributes, traits, and mental
characteristics which are expected to undergo development at college
along with academic learning. It is usual that such items reference the
"whole person" concept and are discussed in terms of the baccalaureate
colleges with the strong implication that this is a main purpose for
college. There is no reason, however, to let the notion develop that a
community college student is any less a "whole person" than a baccalaureate student just because he or she attends a community college which
has a different purpose. Since the two-year student often goes to college
to learn how to do some specific kind of work, to expect him or her to
learn more "general education" than enough to let him function adequately in society while doing occupational or trade work may be an
unreasonable expectation. The two-year and four-year students likely

attend college for different reasons. After equal time of college exposure they know different things but does either have any less total knowledge than the other? In the evaluation of student performance in two-year colleges it would seem that searching for indications of the more so-phisticated attributes or characteristics of general education may be an unrealistic expectation in view of institutional and student purposes.

The general studies component, however, should not be treated lightly, even though it may represent only one-fourth of the program of studies. "Some [industries] have discovered that the kinds of skills provided by a general education are often, in the long run, more valuable to pro-ductivity than those provided by more narrowly focused courses of study" (Ewell 1984, p. 48). Other than the general studies component, though, there is very little uniformity in the programs of study of the two-year students; and comprehensive evaluation of these students, ex-cept incrementally by their course instructors, is difficult.

Evaluating General Education

Evaluation of students' performances in general studies might con-sider using one commercial test—the College Outcome & Measures Project (COMP) developed by the American College Testing Program (ACT). It measures gain that students make in basic skills and knowl-edge shown to be relevant to effective functioning as adults (Noel and Saluri 1983). It is most often used to measure gains between entrance and graduation, but it can be applied over as little as two years of college work (Roueche 1983) and has been used by community colleges as well as by baccalaureate institutions.

Evaluating Courses and Programs

An interesting observation made by Marcus, Leone, and Goldberg (1983) may have relevance for student performance. They discussed the use of alumni survey information in evaluating student satisfaction with college programs and concentrated on those aspects of college education which seemed to be important to future success. They observed that successful alumni had rated communications skills as being the most important aspect, creative problem-solving ability and information gathering and handling skills as being close behind, and that technical knowledge was less important. They were more direct with the state-ment, "In the long run . . . the strongest indicator of student learning

is the relative future success of program graduates, hence the desira-
bility of alumni surveys" (p. 50).

In colleges where currently there is little or no interest in performance
evaluation except on the basis of accomplishments in individual courses,
grades continue to be the incremental measure of educational outcomes;
and grade-point averages (GPAs) are the performance indicators. If the
true concern is for quality education as a preparation for life work, then
this approach may not be a reliable evaluation method. It has been
reported, for example, that "numerous studies going back at least 75
years reveal that there is little or no relationship between grades and
any measures of adult accomplishment" (Milton, Pollio, and Eison 1986,
p. 22). On the other hand, if there is no perceived reason for a deeper
evaluation of student performance, then the course level testing may be
adequate for the colleges that prefer it.

Group discussion, oral presentations, and self-evaluations by the students are among some other evaluation methods that have been found
to be useful, but since these are not quantifying methods of measurement, many others choose not to consider them because of the subjectivity. Pace (1984) observes that people readily accept students' scores
on achievement tests which are objective and tend not to accept profes-
sorial tests because they are believed to be subjective. Pace then says,
"We agree that the 'objective test' is acceptable . . . but that the judgment
of the professor who decided upon its content and who agreed upon its
scoring key, is not acceptable? What a curious confusion" (p. 15). He
also comments on student self-evaluations of learning which people tend
not to believe: "When students say they have not learned much, we
believe them. But when they say they have learned a lot, we do not
believe them. What a commentary that is on our attitudes about students" (ibid.).

Evaluation for Placement

One school of thought views the assessment of students to be primarily
for placement at the outset of their college experience, believing that
not only should their learning be measured, but their abilities and interests, their past performances, readiness, goals, and motivation should
also be evaluated. This early assessment approach tends to promote
extensive developmental education, counseling, and continual reassess-
ment through graduation. It is particularly important in assisting with
remedial programs.

Terminal Evaluation

To assist students in gaining perception of a "real world" connection with the overall college experience, E. Boyer (1986) suggests three steps in one kind of final evaluation: (1) the students be required to write senior theses relating their majors to historical, social, or ethical concerns; (2) have the students present their papers in a senior discussion seminar; and (3) have a select few seniors participate in a public colloquium. While he proposes these steps specifically for students completing their baccalaureate work, the idea could be adapted to two-year graduates. It is not likely that the students involved with occupational programs, in particular, would have either the foundation or the inclination to prepare or present a formal thesis, but the idea of a summative seminar could have merit. A seminar could even be a final course in each of the various programs in which the students would give a report that reviewed their two years of work.

In community colleges where student performance evaluations have the purpose of indicating the effectiveness of that particular system, the use of matrix testing is a method that could be considered. Braskamp, Brandenburg, and Ory (1984, p. 63) point out that information collected from students through the use of matrix sampling, where not all students receive every item but a portion of students receive a portion of the test items, can result in more coverage of the material for a given length of testing time. The tests cannot be used for grading but total time spent taking examinations by students can be reduced. Because of the sampling nature used in this kind of testing, the results are more reliable when used with large homogenous groups where there can be confidence that the samples are representative of the whole population.

Staffing for Assessment

Lenning (1977) suggests that each community college should have a person and an office on campus devoted to keeping up with assessment developments and available to counsel faculty in the development and use of assessment instruments and data. This suggestion serves to point out the kind of attention that should be given to the matter of evaluating student performance; however, many community colleges do not place sufficient priority on this operation to adequately fund and staff such an office. Some larger colleges have moved in this direction.

Before deciding on an approach or an evaluation instrument for student performance, colleges need to consider many factors. Developing one's own instrument of student evaluation is as feasible as using one that is commercially available. Even so, there are advantages to examining the assessment tools and examples that others have generated rather than starting from scratch (Ewell 1985a). If a college decides to use a commercially available performance assessment instrument, a review of Ewell (1983, 40-41), may be helpful.

The Florida Approach

In Florida, where a statewide comprehensive system of competency-based eduction and assessment has been in place since 1976, the College-Level Academic Skills Test (CLAST) is given to students at the end of their sophomore year. McTarnaghan (1986) points out that CLAST measures communication and computation skills that all students are expected to master by that time. Earlier, the CLAST scores were used only for counseling, but since 1984 the associate of arts degree students must meet a minimum CLAST score to graduate. McTarnaghan writes that the competency program has been successful in improving student achievement. The purpose of the program is to improve instruction and student performance, and the faculty generally support it. Blee (1985) notes that the content and methodology of the competency tests are in harmony with the content and methodology of the instructional programs, thus making it a sound evaluation approach. Nickens (1985), however, notes that there is an inclination to set up, for admission to programs, criteria which lead to the exit exam. "The clientele for which the institution was brought into existence to serve in the first place— low socioeconomic, the deprived, and the adult seeking economic mobility—may never get past remediation . . . because they cannot meet the criteria for placement [in these programs]" (p. 53). Nickens observes that because of the time between program delivery and assessment, exit testing has little value toward instructional improvement, and little value to the student. The Florida program will need additional time before it can be evaluated comprehensively.

The Georgia Approach

Georgia has a similar program, known as "rising junior exam," which requires individual students to demonstrate mastery of "college level skills" before they can advance beyond the sophomore year (Ewell 1987). Other states have mounted a variety of initiatives aimed at improving the quality of undergraduate education in public colleges. C. Boyer and McGuinness (1986) write that "state action, even though relatively blunt at times, is stimulating public colleges and universities to scrutinize their undergraduate programs and to undertake their own renewal and reform" (p. 12). Their tabulation of the various state initiatives can help the reader to gain a larger perspective on state level mandates.

Value-Added Evaluation

The second fundamental type of student assessment mentioned previously, value-added evaluation, considers the developmental process that occurs within a student as the result of an educational experience. To positively affect the students' abilities, attitudes, and knowledge is the goal of a quality institution. "The highest quality institutions, in this view, are those that have the greatest impact—add the most value—to the students' knowledge, personality, and career development" (A. Astin 1982, p. 11).

While value-added evaluation may be used to assess institutions, programs, and students, the focus here is upon its value in evaluating individual student performance. Most student performance evaluations focus on the assessment of each student and then compare that performance against some normative standard. The value-added approach, however, provides feedback to students, faculty, and administrators on the levels of learning mastery and the degree to which they change over time.

Value-added assessment first identifies a set of measurement processes that evaluate a student's performance compared to some desired outcome. These processes may include a nationally normed test such as ACT's COMP, a questionnaire, a summative thesis, or observed performance. The focus is not on how or what data is collected, but it is on the process of interpreting the data in regard to individual student development. These data can be used to assess progress as well as strengths and weaknesses, to plan curricular choices, and to direct effort toward the desired learning goals for the individual student.

Use of the value-added evaluation approach thus far has been limited almost exclusively to the baccalaureate institutions; however, the two-year community and technical colleges may be the ideal sites for this approach. In selective four-year colleges and universities the student body is relatively homogeneous and above average in ability. Two-year institutions, however, accept a more heterogeneous group of students who have a wide range of abilities. In examining the personal development of the two-year graduates, it is likely that many have progressed farther proportionally than their four-year counterparts. Considering the value added to these students' lives as a result of their education experience, the two-year institutions can compete with and often excel in comparison to their baccalaureate counterparts.

Northeast Missouri State University's Approach

Both two-year and four-year institutions desiring to undertake the value-added evaluation approach would benefit from studying the following steps which were taken at Northeast Missouri State University. (American Association of State Colleges and Universities, 1984):

Step 1. Possess clear goals and objectives. The assessment of student progress, being crucial to the learning enterprise, should be reflected in the overall goals and objectives of the college or university. From the broad mission statement to specific student objectives, the evaluation concept should be reflected.

Step 2. Develop adequately advanced capacity to collect data and monitor student progress. The evaluation of student performance requires a relatively sophisticated data collection, maintenance, and analysis capacity. Monitoring student progress entails data collection at many points in (and after) the education experience. The maintenance and manipulation of the data collected is relatively complex and requires adequate resources in staff and equipment to properly conduct the project.

Step 3. Decide upon an evaluation strategy. The selection of appropriate evaluation methods and strategy is implemented in the success of any assessment process. Critical to the value-added approach is the capacity to assess the entry-level and the exit-level performance of each student. Thus, the relative progress can be measured and made available. The range of available assessment strategies include the ACT and the SAT, the College Outcome & Measures Project, the ACT Residuals Exam, institutionally designed tests, observational measures, and surveys. It might be a good strategy to use a "Multi-dimensional Approach" (Moden and Williford 1987), which does not depend upon any one measure.

Step 4. Implement the process. Astin has pointed out that the value-added process is a "time-consuming, expensive, and potentially decisive method of assessing quality" (1982, p. 10). Implementing a value-added system should be undertaken with the seriousness it deserves. As with any significant educational change, the process needs to begin with a commitment at the top. The chief executive officer (CEO), the governing board, and other leaders of the institution need to wholeheartedly support the project. The current movement by some states to require the use of a value-added evaluation process may prove counterproductive if the leadership of the institution is not in agreement with the body requiring the evaluation. E. Boyer warns "against accepting yardsticks shaped by politicians rather than those who know most about what goes on in a university" (Fiske 1987, p. 1).

The two-year college personnel who are considering the value-added evaluation process should do a careful cost study. Assessing, processing, analyzing, reporting, and acting on the results of assessment can be costly in materials and equipment, time, and personnel. The implementation of value-added evaluation for some institutions may be cost prohibitive.

There is a debate about the extent that value-added assessment should be used for the evaluation of student learning. Manning (1987) calls for the use of value-added concepts only for programmatic and institutional evaluation; students should be assessed, "primarily on the level of competency, understanding, or proficiency they attain" (p. 52). Manning also cautions that the value-added approach presumes that educational growth is an additive process when much evidence suggests that learning is more likely to be a re-structuring of the underlying components of knowledge. Thus the pre-test/post-test approach is not measuring the "addition" of any value but rather the redesigning of that which is acquired (ibid.). Additional practical considerations, such as the lack of standardized evaluation instruments in various technical fields, may preclude or limit the utilization of the value-added approach in two-year colleges.

Effective Student Performance Assessment

Regardless of the procedural details, it is suggested that every student performance assessment should contain most of the following characteristics:

1. Examines a variety of student outcomes. Both a competency-based and a value-added component may be utilized, and no *one* outcome should be considered the best or only measure.
2. Utilizes a variety of techniques such as written examinations, observational data, and oral presentations. Variety allows for the

differences in individual learning and assessment styles and the varying interests of different institutions.

3. Is performed at different times and with different procedures. Again, this variety allows for individual learning differences.

4. Is not used solely as an instrument for comparing students for determining grades. Student evaluation should be a part of a system that measures the student's progress toward predetermined goals. Assessment measures should be shared with the student and utilized by both the evaluator and the student as guides toward further educational experiences.

In developing a plan for evaluating student performance, a number of components can be examined. A stated purpose, and local assessment development and/or adaptations are essential. Beyond that, each campus will have to determine for itself what resources it can devote to the evaluation, what data are desired, how the data will be developed, and how the data will be used.

3

Evaluating Full-Time Faculty Members

*By Robert L. Cherry, Peter H. Grant
and Katherine D. Kalinos*

E valuation processes have a long history in education. Bloom
(1987) makes two points about Socrates' views on evaluation.
First, Socrates accepts the right of the Athenians to make an
evaluation, and second, "He only wants to be left alone" (p. 266). These
two statements also express faculty views toward evaluation. They accept
the process intellectually, but they, too, want to be left alone as much as
possible.

Evaluation for appraising the effectiveness of an employee is summative evaluation. Encouragement is given in enhancing those talents
that are basic foundations on which successful careers are built; therefore, evaluation is also formative—used to improve competence.

The evaluation process should be built on procedures which are governed by acknowledging that the "relationship between faculty and their
institution is . . . far less one of 'understanding' and 'custom,' and far
more on articulated rules" (Wright 1985, p. 370). One of the rules is
that the faculty should be apprised of the uses of the evaluation results
and they should receive feedback for professional development. Without
systematic feedback the evaluative system becomes less effective. Instructional skills can be enhanced by positive feedback or a different
instructional style may be adopted which improves the teaching process.

What Are We Evaluating?

Since teaching is the highest educational priority of two-year college faculty and administrators, the evaluation of instruction is an integral part of the collegiate enterprise. The essence of the instructional evaluation process is to provide help for faculty to examine their teaching for improving instruction ultimately for the benefit of students (League for Innovation in Community Colleges 1985). It also assists administrative personnel in making enlightened decisions concerning status of faculty, considering such items as pay adjustments, promotion, and tenure.

Instructional evaluation and its processes are institutional matters and adequate importance needs to be devoted to the system. Proper credibility should be directed to the process which can result in a proper trust relationship (Guba and Lincoln 1981). In discussing assessment techniques, Arreola indicates that faculty "viewed the process with a degree of apprehension, suspicion, fear, anxiety, resentfulness, and hostility" (1983, p. 85). The criteria used to evaluate instruction and the complexities of teaching activities should be fairly represented in any finalized documents. Case studies show that faculty morale with regard to evaluation tends to be highest where procedures are established and well known (Moomaw 1977). Evaluation is as much a social and human activity as it is a technical activity.

Validity of Evaluation

The validity of the evaluation process, particularly self-evaluations, has been questioned over the years. "Research on self-evaluation for either professional improvement or for personnel decisions is spotty in quality and short in quantity" (Miller 1987, p. 84). Miller also cites research and the relevance of the findings and states that valid evaluations take all relevant variables into account and judges them objectively. One can find research to validate their desires relative to having or not having a system of instructional evaluation. How long can an individual institution operate effectively without having some such system?

Grasha states that instructional methods may be more effective than instructor characteristics in influencing student learning, stating, "other things beside content achievement are potentially legitimate classroom outcomes and that evaluation of content and non-content should focus on the adequacy of the methods for meeting the obtained goals" (1977, p. 29).

Self-Evaluation

Two-year colleges, emphasizing the teaching function, strive to provide their students with the most effective instructors and teaching methods. Evaluation should be an integral part of the overall developmental plan of the college and self-evaluation is a necessary component of the instructional evaluation process (M. Boyer 1973).

Self-evaluations, ranging from informal self-reflections to formal written appraisals presented to supervisors or peers, can be a valuable source of information. The results of the process can provide benefits by systematically analyzing what and how one teaches. Braskamp, Brandenburg, and Ory (1984) recommend the inclusion of items ranging from courses taught and learning outcomes to community involvement and colleague evaluations.

The self-evaluation process as a prescribed element in personnel decisions is not generally used although the care and typing of personnel files becomes a *de facto* self-evaluation and should be recognized as such by those involved in presenting files for personnel decisions. Some institutions do use descriptions of teaching, philosophy, and academic load, as input elements for the summative phase of the evaluation process. Self-evaluation of teaching may provide contextual information for assessing teaching effectiveness while descriptions of accomplishments and future goals can provide a useful framework for evaluating the total instructional performance of an instructor.

For formative purposes, self-evaluations can be compared with student evaluations if the same items are administered to the students. Research findings indicate that students and instructors show good relative agreement on overall ratings of an instructor. Teachers rated highly by students have been shown to rate themselves higher than teachers who are rated less highly by students. It also has been found that teacher self-ratings and student ratings on specific dimensions of student involvement, teacher support, and instructional skill are the most congruent. Other studies have also recognized that instructor self-ratings are not unduly influenced by the instructor's age, sex, tenure status, teaching load, or years of teaching experience (Braskamp et al., 1984; Miller 1987).

Faculty can also increase the utility of their self-evaluation by discussing the evaluation with faculty colleagues or a staff member responsible for faculty development. This kind of feedback can be helpful. Faculty members wishing to focus on specific classroom teaching behavior should consider using aids such as videotaping a lecture or a discussion and using a self-administered rating scale. M. Boyer indicates that videotaping could be a valuable tool in producing increasingly better instructors (1973). Audio and video recordings can be used to help one see the teaching act as others see it. However, video taping is not for everyone, and its effectiveness varies with the subject. Those subjects that lend themselves to lecturing and to sequential presentations are captured more easily on film than are subjects that involve more discussion.

The Administrator's Role

Andrews indicates that he "believes strongly that excellence can and must be expected but cannot be assumed without an effective administrative evaluation system for faculty" (1985, pp. vi-vii). From a faculty perspective there is concern with the administrative role in evaluation, and the possible misuse of power. Administrators have an institutional responsibility in the summative evaluation process and ultimately to play the major role. Moomaw indicates that survey results in two-year institutions show that the principal responsibility for evaluation usually belongs to the academic dean or vice-president for academic affairs (1977).

A report from the National Institute of Education (1984, p. 57) indicates that "in changing current systems of assessment, academic administrators and faculty should ensure that the instruments and methods used are appropriate for (1) the knowledge, capacities, and skills addressed and (2) the stated objectives of undergraduate education at their institutions." Administrators are expected to implement policy—a policy which should involve those who are affected by it. Administrators need to approach the process with an open mind and be willing to develop other methods. There is generally more than one means to solve a problem. Cronbach observes that parties having divergent perceptions and aims bear down on administrators as they maneuver toward a politically acceptable accommodation (1980).

Instructional Methods

Grasha indicates that instructional methods may be more effective than instructor characteristics in influencing student learning. His position may be summarized by stating, "Other things beside content achievement are potentially legitimate classroom outcomes and evaluation of content and non-content should focus on the adequacy of the methods for meeting the obtained goals" (1977, p. 29).

Some excellent work has been done at the two-year college level on instructional evaluation. The ACCTion Consortium conducted a project which dealt with developing systems of evaluation for two-year colleges. The Consortium developed a number of documents, including the Teaching Faculty Perception Inventories (1983) and Master Teacher Assessment and Professional Growth (1982) forms. The Faculty Perception Inventories are designed to reflect perceptions about performance in relation to professional responsibilities based on a number of factors, including professional characteristics, learning environment, evaluation activities, course development, advising/counseling activities, and administrative type-clerical functions. Seventy-three variables are contained in this set of inventories, covering self, supervisory, and colleague forms along with a professional development plan.

The Master Teacher form lists the following nine competencies: possess and exhibit personal characteristics, exhibit professional behavior, use the problem-solving process, communicate effectively, use interpersonal skills, plan/organize learning experiences, facilitate student learning, evaluate students, and stimulate lifelong learning. Including supporting skills, the items number 76. These forms can assist in planning professional growth activities and developing new skills.

Herrscher (1976) developed an Instructional Effectiveness Inventory with 60 items which focuses on instructional design, accommodating individual differences, and educational competencies and goals. It can be used to identify specific areas where change might be needed in a course and to allow supervisors to assess an instructor's effectiveness.

Goodwin and Smith (1985) present a method that assists in developing an evaluation system beginning with a basic philosophy in Phase 1. The authors provide a variety of worksheets that can facilitate adapting an evaluation system that can be compatible to specific institutional purposes. Format alternatives as well as semantic differences are accommodated and discussed in the book. Specific options concerning evaluation items are presented in categories ranging alphabetically from accounting and analytical ability to the categories of thoughtfulness and work habits.

Student Evaluations of Teaching

Students evaluate teachers throughout their passage from kindergarten to high school graduation, and parents unconsciously encourage evaluation by asking their primary school aged children "what happened at school today?" High school students also compare the performances of their teachers. By the time students reach a college classroom they are experienced observers of teaching.

Student evaluations of college teaching are common, yet the concept of students evaluating college faculty is not a universally held virtue. In a letter to *The Chronicle of Higher Education* (October 14, 1987), Cahn questioned the validity of student evaluations of faculty, claiming such activity to be inappropriate and dangerous. Cahn maintained that

> Students, by definition, do not know the subject matter they are studying, and so they are in a poor position to judge whether it is being taught well or whether the instructor's presentation is shallow, inaccurate, incomplete, or biased. Students know if teachers are likable, not if they are knowledgeable; students know if lectures are enjoyable, not if they are reliable (p. B-2).

Cahn's views represent a view of the minority of faculty members; well over 60 percent of faculty members, according to national evidence, favor the prudent use of student evaluations of teaching, and the two-year college faculty acceptance rate is closer to 90 percent. Young and Gwalamubisi (1986) cite a study of community college faculty in Washington which indicates that student ratings of faculty are the most commonly used form of evaluation as well as the most desired form of evaluation. Centra (1979) found that 90 percent of the 326 two-year colleges responding used student ratings as a part of faculty evaluation.

The responsibilities of college faculty members may include research, advising, committee work, public service, and service to the college, as well as teaching. The major responsibility in two-year colleges is teaching students in the classroom, and the methods of evaluating faculty performance vary just as faculty responsibilities vary. Since the major responsibility of faculty members is instruction, the major component of evaluating faculty performance involves assessing instructional activities; therefore, student ratings of faculty are an important ingredient in any faculty evaluation process.

While students spend a great deal of time observing and reacting to faculty, it is important to focus student evaluations on areas in which they are competent to judge. Miller writes that the areas of teaching that students are best able to evaluate are "pedagogical effectiveness; evaluation fairness; interest in the student; interest in the subject; and course organization" (1987, p. 54). Centra (1979) cites several studies in establishing a list of dimensions or items commonly appearing on student evaluation forms. The three most commonly displayed are (1) organization, structure, or clarity; (2) teacher-student interaction or rapport; and (3) teaching skill, communication, or lecturing ability. Other categories included occasionally in rating instruments are evaluations of the course workload or difficulty, grading and examinations, impact on students (self-rated student accomplishment), and global or overall effectiveness. Braskamp et al. state that "students are appropriate sources when they are describing or judging student-instructor relationships, their views of the instructor's professional and ethical behavior, their workload, what they have learned in the course, fairness of grading, and instructor's ability to communicate" (1984, pp. 36-38).

The features of the rating instrument also need to be considered. Major areas of instructional effectiveness, such as communication skill and course organization, may be assessed, or students may be asked to rate their progress in a number of course objectives. Another approach is the "cafeteria" form, where faculty members select items from a pool that are most relevant in evaluating their course. All types of rating forms should be flexible enough to accommodate a variety of teaching styles; they should contain clear and concise instructions, and be limited to one page (Andrews 1985; Braskamp et al. 1984; Centra 1979; Miller 1974).

There is general agreement in the literature that student ratings of faculty teaching can produce consistently reliable and valid results provided enough students have made ratings. Agreement among students on global ratings—comparing faculty to their peers—is sufficiently high if the class has over 15 students. Those ratings are consistent even if given at different times during the term. The instructional performance assessment can be trusted if the student sample includes five or more classes with at least 15 students in each class. It is important to note, however, that personnel decisions should be based upon an instructor's performance in several courses (Braskamp et al., 1984; Cashin 1983; Centra 1979; Gilmore, Kane, and Naccarato 1978).

The process of evaluation normally raises concern on the part of those being evaluated, and Cashin (1983) has identified three concerns regarding student ratings in community colleges. These are (1) the use of comparative data, (2) the reading level of the student raters, and (3) the rating of skill courses. When standardized rating systems are used, community college faculty receive higher ratings than four-year college faculty. Cashin speculates that this finding is due to the emphasis community colleges place on teaching. While this finding may not seem to be a problem, if only community college evaluation data from *standardized* systems are used, percentile scores for individual instructors will be lower due to higher overall norms. Finally, the standardized rating forms in general use are not designed for evaluating the skill courses that are found in vocational-technical programs. Cashin writes: "The present state of our knowledge about which teaching behaviors lead to student learning in such courses is very limited, and so little concrete advice can be offered" (ibid, p. 64).

Colleague Evaluation

While students can judge fairly and perceptively certain aspects of faculty performance if the right questions are asked, some areas are best judged by other faculty members. An instructor's knowledge of a particular field, the selection of course objectives, class assignments, student achievement, departmental activities, research, and instructional style are among those items best rated by colleagues (Braskamp et al., 1984; Cohen and McKeachie 1980).

Colleague evaluations, by themselves, may be of little use in personnel decisions but in summative evaluations of teaching, colleague evaluations can have utility (Centra 1975; and Cohen and McKeachie 1980). The quality of teaching effectiveness can be rated by colleagues, who can focus on knowledge of subject matter, commitment to teaching, or the qualities of good teaching. Colleagues can also judge the course design and instructional materials of a particular instructor. They can assess student achievement and also integrate information from a variety of sources regarding the circumstances under which instruction occurs (Cohen and McKeachie 1980). Centra identifies several features of teaching that colleagues can adequately evaluate for both formative and summative purposes, including the qualifications and subject knowledge of the instructor, the course syllabus, objectives, reading list and materials, the assignments and examinations, and perhaps student achievement.

Braskamp et al. (1984) discuss concerns for the relevance of classroom visits for peer evaluation, particularly for personnel decisions. They offer several generalizations regarding classroom observations, including a concern for the effect that an observer in the classroom may have on the teaching-learning process, a lack of agreement between colleagues regarding instructor effectiveness, and the lack of agreement between colleague ratings and student ratings where colleague ratings of faculty performance are higher than those of students.

Classroom observations are not necessary to assess overall faculty performance. Faculty members have numerous opportunities in departmental meetings, committee meetings, and team-teaching experiences to observe their colleagues' contributions to the learning environment. To help assess the contribution to student learning, a review of instructional materials by a colleague of the same academic background may be useful (Centra 1975; Hoyt 1982).

The validity of colleague ratings is an important concern for evaluators. Centra (1979) cites a study conducted at a new institution where faculty members were evaluated on two different occasions by each of three colleagues for a total of six different ratings. Ninety-four percent of the responses of rating overall instructor effectiveness were either excellent or good, and student ratings were favorable but they were not as high as those by faculty members. The reliability of colleague ratings was further tarnished by an average correlation among different colleagues of .26. In a study of 52 community college faculty members, Fitzgerald and Grafton (1981) compared responses by students and peers in assessing classroom performance. They found that peer ratings were somewhat higher than student ratings but that the differences were not significant. In comparison to student ratings, the use of colleague evaluations has not been extensive in recent years (Cohen and McKeachie 1980). Centra (1979) estimated that 27 percent of the two-year colleges use colleague evaluations to formally assess at least one-half of their faculty while 34 percent make no use of colleague evaluations. Additional evidence on these and other evaluation issues is included in the compendium, *Key Resources on Community Colleges*, by Cohen, Palmer, and Zwemer (1986).

Growth Contracts

Evaluation systems frequently focus on one specific form of evaluation, such as student ratings or colleague ratings. An exception to this phenomena is the growth contract system, which is a variation of the Management By Objectives (MBO) concept which ties individual development to the needs of the college (Stroup 1983). In this approach the faculty member being assessed and the evaluators form a team, and strengths and weaknesses are assessed through observations and analysis. The team seeks to assist in the improvement of the individual faculty member rather than make a definitive judgment about that person's abilities (Moomaw 1977).

This type of evaluation is used primarily for formative evaluations with a separate summative process for personnel decisions. Among the benefits of growth contracts are emphasis and responsibility placed on the individual, and its flexible and systematic nature. It focuses on diagnosis and development at regular intervals. Twenty-three percent of the two-year colleges used growth contracts with over 50 percent of their faculty some 10-15 years ago; and 71 percent of the two-year colleges indicate that growth contracts are effective or very effective (Centra 1979; Moomaw 1977). Current data are not available.

Appeal and Grievance Procedures

Administrators and faculty need protection from unlawful or illegal practices. An appeal and grievance procedure allows the faculty member to address what is perceived to be an unfair practice by the administration. The same process helps protect the administration from lawsuits concerning the due process clause of the Fourteenth Amendment. Kaplan (1986) has cited a considerable number of lawsuits which are relevant to higher education. The two cases considered landmark decisions by the Supreme Court are *Board of Regents v. Roth* 408 U.S. 564 (1972) and *Perry v. Sinderman* 408 U.S. 593 (1972). These cases, "established that faculty members have a right to a fair hearing whenever a personnel decision deprives them of a 'property interest' or a 'liberty interest' under the Fourteenth Amendment's due process clause" (Kaplan 1986, p. 168).

The appeal and grievance procedure should be developed with the advice of an attorney. Leslie and Satryb list six "basic elements of a grievance procedure."

1. The *scope* addresses the question of what is grievable.
2. The *structure* may have as few as one step to as many as eight steps.
3. *Access* defines who has the right to grieve under the procedure.
4. *Powers of remedy* confers the power "to restore to the grievant his property or liberties . . ." (p. 194).
5. *Procedure elements* have several components, including time limits. Initiation of the process "must normally be undertaken within a specified period" and "time limits are normally placed on all phases of the procedure" (1977, p. 192-195).
6. *Delegation of power to resolve grievances* is complex and needs to be studied carefully.

There are both informal and formal grievance procedures. The informal procedure may begin when a grievant faculty member has a discussion with his or her supervisor. If this procedure is unsatisfactory, the next supervisory level is contacted and, with both parties in attendance, an oral presentation is made. If the grievant faculty has reservations about discussing the problem with the immediate supervisor, he or she may discuss the dispute with the next higher level supervisor. If the dispute remains unresolved, a formal grievance procedure may be instituted.

Some institutions have a faculty grievance officer who acts informally to resolve disputes. The grievance officer may review the situation with the faculty member and then approach the first level supervisor or may offer advice against pursuing the matter further it is without merit (Larrowe 1986).

The formal procedure should have clearly stated rules concerning the selection of the person or persons who will make the recommendation for resolution of the dispute. If a panel is to mediate, there should be a definition as to who is eligible to serve and how the selection is made. It is not uncommon for the administration to name one or two individuals and the grievant to name the same number. This group may choose another individual to prevent a deadlock. In another method, an administrator, such as the dean of faculty or the vice president of academic affairs, is designated as the chairperson and will select one other member; and the grievant will select one other member. The process should be known well in advance and clearly articulated.

Written communications are to be exchanged for each step of the process; panel members and the grievant are notified in writing as to the time and date of the meetings and each due date is specified by a calendar date. Time limits are imposed to prevent foot-dragging by either side in the dispute, although this circumstance may occur when the time limit is extended to its maximum (BNA Editorial Staff, 1972).

The grievant should have the right to some type of representation; usually another faculty member serves in this capacity at this stage. Evidence between the grievant and the panel is exchanged in written form, and the procedure includes to whom the panel will submit its recommendation—usually the CEO. The grievant has a right to a copy of the recommendation and a right to submit a written objection to the individual making the final decision. When the decision is made, the grievant has a right to this knowledge and to make an appeal to the board of trustees, unless the process has taken place under binding arbitration. By using the institutional process the grievant does not forfeit the right to institute legal action.

The importance of the decision-making procedure is commented on by Hendrickson and Lee who state: "Frequently, a court will agree to review decision-making procedures but declare the substance of a decision and its supporting criteria unreviewable because such matters are within the discretion of organizational decision makers" (1983, p. 28).

The courts generally have taken the stance that decisions within academia are not in their purview if the procedures are in compliance with the due process clause of the Fourteenth Amendment.

Summary

Faculty evaluation is here to stay. Each institution should develop or purchase a model which best suits its needs and philosophy. It is not always feasible to install another institution's model since it may not take into consideration the special needs or aspects of your institution, but there are standardized models that may be modified to meet particularized interests and needs. For a detailed listing of several nationally used models for student evaluation of classroom teaching, see Appendix A in Miller, 1987.

The evaluation policies and procedures used should be developed by a joint effort of administration and faculty. When the evaluative procedures are in place, care needs to be taken that they are used in a timely manner for all concerned parties. It is important that formative and summative purposes of evaluation be understood by both the faculty and administration, and that there is a grievance or appeal procedure for disputes which may arise.

4

Evaluating Part-Time Faculty Members

By Corrine M. Brown and Lynn M. Rector

During the past decade, faculty evaluation has gained support and acceptance as the trend toward accountability focused on the academic community. "While faculty evaluation was gaining institutional acceptance, a second phenomenon of the decade was being recognized. Community colleges were employing increasing numbers of part-time faculty" (Behrendt and Parsons 1983, p. 34). The literature supports the view that as the numbers of part-time faculty increase, the implementation of systematic and integrated evaluation systems for part-time faculty becomes more important.

Formulating a Definition

Each institution needs to formulate a definition of "part-time," that will be administratively useful for the individual institution. Gappa (1984, p. 5) defines part-time faculty as anyone who (1) teaches less than the average full-time teaching load, or (2) has less than a full-time faculty assignment and range of duties, or (3) may have a temporary full-time assignment. The definition of what constitutes part-time is not as simple as in the case of full-time, and will vary among institutions accordingly. Since there are different categories of part-timers, it follows that several evaluation systems might be established. However, one underlying concept will always be present; the evaluation system will aim at improving upon or maintaining existing levels of teaching effectiveness and defining clear standards of performance for part-time faculty.

Part-Time Faculty: Pro and Con

Community colleges must respond to constantly changing economic, social, and political environments. Boggs (1984, p. 5) writes:

> To survive, community colleges must be able to respond to financial constraints, new demands, and enrollment patterns on a term-by-term basis. One of the most hotly debated responses to uncertainty has been the increased utilization of part-time or adjunct instructors.

The use of part-time faculty allows flexibility in course offerings as well as course scheduling and off-campus offerings. Part-time faculty typically teach at hours that are undesirable to the full-time faculty, and they teach for less pay and few, if any, fringe benefits. In examining reasons for the increased use of part-time faculty, Seldin (1984, p. 12) writes that "since higher education is a labor-intensive industry, with 70 to 80 percent of most budgets going for salaries, it was inevitable for the instructional staff to be regarded as one of the first areas to be pruned. A large number of colleges and universities neatly avoided the high salaries and fringe benefits of full-time faculty by hiring lower-salaried, few-or-no-benefit, part-time instructors." As Boggs notes, "the financial incentive for employment of part-time faculty is obviously strong" (1984, p. 9).

In contrast to the financial advantages associated with the use of part-time faculty, there are also a number of problems or concerns. A major problem is acceptance. Leslie and others (1982, p. 5) note that full-timers view part-timers as an economic and political threat to their security and well being. Part-timers are viewed as contributing very little, if anything, to the institution beyond teaching their courses. Tuckman (1978, p. 307) reported that only 40 percent of part-time faculty participate in curriculum development, presumably because they have a full-time commitment elsewhere and generally are not interested in such assignments. However, curriculum meetings usually are held during "normal" working hours, which excludes part-time faculty who hold other jobs. If an institution is to take full advantage of its part-time faculty, then it needs to explore ways to involve them in course development and to increase their interaction with full-timers.

Little, if any, interaction between part-time and full-time faculty exists in many institutions. Kellams and Kyre (1978, p. 33) reported that only 26 percent of the part-time faculty interact socially with full-timers. In many institutions, part-timers are committed to using course outlines and syllabi that are developed by someone else. If material on the syllabus is not covered, or is covered differently by the part-timer, allegations of poor instructional quality may be made. Boggs (1984, p. 11) notes that "few studies have been conducted to determine whether students taught by part-time faculty receive instruction inferior to that offered by full-time instructors. Research based mainly on student ratings reveals no statistical difference."

Part-Time Faculty Evaluation

Perhaps this feeling of complacency towards part-time faculty explains why there are few integrated evaluation systems for part-timers. Many institutions administer student evaluations for their part-time faculty, but the use of student evaluations alone does not make an integrated evaluation system. A systematic evaluation procedure contains various components so that evaluation data is gathered from multiple sources. Boggs (1984, p. 12) goes further in claiming that "in most settings, evaluation simply does not occur or is in need of radical revision." A review of the literature supports the statement that systematic and integrated evaluation systems for part-time faculty are not common. The effective and systematic evaluation of part-time faculty should be a specific institutional priority for responsible educational practice. "Part-timers have contact with a large percentage of the student population. Evaluation of their performance is critical" (Bramlett and Rodriquez 1982-83, p. 41).

Some institutions have addressed the evaluation of part-time faculty by using the evaluation system that is used for full-time faculty. These evaluation systems may not distinguish the special needs or recognize the unique contributions of part-timers. Full-time evaluation systems are used primarily for promotion and tenure decision issues, which rarely affect part-time faculty. Performance on committees, publications, presentations, and community service, are common full-time faculty criteria that do not apply to part-time faculty members. Since part-timers are employed to teach, teaching effectiveness should be at the core of a part-time evaluation system. Biles and Tuckman (1986, p. 10) contend that institutions that establish personnel policies for part-timers by following the policies for full-timers will limit management flexibility.

They suggest that separate policies should be established for full-timers and part-timers.

Many institutions, unable to formulate one clear, consistent policy for the diverse needs of part-timers, rely on casual agreements rather than systematic evaluation. But as noted by Leslie "casual agreements can lead to misunderstanding, discrimination, unexpected liabilities, and litigation" (1984, p. 12). No employee, including a part-timer, can be dismissed during the term of a contract except for cause. Poor instruction can be just cause, but evidence of poor performance must be documented. The courts are unlikely to accept perceptions and intuition as documentation. Institutional policies can be written to accommodate the varied needs of part-timers and yet be consistent with educational objectives and remain within the law.

Establishing one policy for *all* part-time faculty is not recommended, considering the wide range of people, employment conditions, and expectations involved. As Biles and Tuckman note, "part-timers differ in terms of their motivations for being part-time and, as a consequence, in what they expect from their employing institution. This makes it difficult to formulate a single policy that meets the needs of all of the part-timers employed at that institution" (1986, p. 10).

Methods of Evaluation

The evaluation techniques most often cited for assessing teaching effectiveness are student evaluation, peer (colleague) evaluation, department chair evaluation, self assessment, student learning, growth contracts, and video taping. Of these methods, the department chair, student, and peer evaluation have been judged most effective for full-time faculty (Centra 1979, p. 7). The part-time evaluation system should include an integration of the three methods.

There are two additional methods that may be useful for part-time faculty, given their irregular hours and off-campus locations. Video taping can be a valuable technique to review their classroom performance. Depending upon the teaching experience of the instructor, either one or two taping sessions could be scheduled per term. The department chair or an experienced faculty member would view the tape with the part-time instructor and evaluate the classroom teaching techniques. Any suggestions for improvement would be made at this joint meeting. According to Centra (1979), video taping "has the potential to help and to harm" (p. 55) due to its threatening effect on some faculty. This technique yields the most benefits when the video tape is reviewed with a mentor so the focus is on improvement of delivery skills.

Another suggestion is that of assigning an experienced full-time faculty member to serve as a lead teacher or mentor to the part-time faculty member (Sillman 1980, p. 94). Through the mentor, the part-time faculty member would have the opportunity to interact with full-time faculty, learn about the institution, and receive any needed assistance in improving instructional design and/or delivery skills.

What Should Be Evaluated

Part-timers want to teach, and that is the primary reason institutions hire them; therefore, the focus of the evaluation system for part-timers should be on teaching effectiveness with additional evaluation items being included as they assume other duties, or make other contributions to the institution. Seldin (1984, p. 82) describes teaching "as encompassing three broad dimensions: content expertise, instructional delivery skills, and instructional design skills." These three dimensions provide a solid foundation upon which to develop an evaluation system for teaching effectiveness.

Content Expertise

Content expertise encompasses skills, competencies and mastery in a particular area. Students are not in the best position to evaluate mastery of content, although a question along these lines is often included in student rating surveys. Peer or mentor evaluation would be a more appropriate evaluation technique for gathering information on content expertise. Techniques used could include, classroom visitation, review of video taped class sessions, or the inclusion of part-timers in formal discussions of curriculum and course content.

Instructional Design Skills

Instructional design skills can be divided into two parts (Seldin 1984). The first one may consist of designing and sequencing instructional experiences to induce learning; and the second may consist of being able to measure that learning has occurred. Components are course syllabi, instructional materials, course or lesson objectives, and evaluation or testing methods. This component is most effectively evaluated by a peer, mentor, or department chair.

An instructional design component, however, is not always appropriate when evaluating part-timers. In some institutions, part-timers do not assist in the design of instructional materials, while other colleges expect part-timers to design and to prepare instructional materials, with little or no support services provided by the institution. A part-timer who is involved in the design and preparation of materials should be evaluated on instructional design if it relates to those materials. If meager support services are provided to part-timers, the instructional design materials may be evaluated for content but not on form, style, or medium of presentation.

Delivery Skills

Instructional delivery skills are defined by Seldin "as those human interactive skills and characteristics that promote or facilitate learning by creating an appropriate learning environment" (1984, p. 83). Students are in a unique position to accurately evaluate a faculty member's teaching skills. Generally speaking, student ratings in the area of delivery skills are reliable and valid (ibid.). Student evaluations are a key component in the evaluation system, but they cannot be the only component. Chair evaluation, which may include structured and planned classroom visitations, also can provide first hand knowledge of instructional delivery skills and classroom management techniques.

Behrendt and Parsons (1983) suggest that self-evaluation be included in the part-time evaluation system. Self evaluation allows the instructor to focus on his or her own classroom activities. As Centra (1979) notes, "self analysis is especially important in developing a professional and personal growth plan because it depends on an accurate scrutiny of one's strengths and weaknesses" (1979, p. 48).

Other Criteria To Be Evaluated

An institution should consider evaluating part-time faculty on other factors in addition to classroom teaching. Two prominent criteria are personal attributes and service contributions.

Personal Attributes

Does the part-time instructor bring prestige to the institution? Perhaps a part-timer's unique position in the community or recognition as an authority in a specific content area will benefit the institution.

Does the part-timer afford the institution with an important contact in a college-industry connection? As mentioned in chapter eight, industrial and external relations are increasingly important to educational institutions. The use of certain part-time faculty could be the focal point of this important linkage.

How long has the individual been employed by the institution? While some part-timers are only employed for one term, others have been employed with the same institution for many years. Their continued employment could indicate that they make an important contribution to the institution.

Service Contributions

Does the individual participate in college or departmental committees? Given the opportunity, some part-timers are eager to participate, especially on committees involving curriculum and course content.

Does the part-timer provide advising to students? Students seek advice on career goals and employment opportunities from part-timers. This relationship is especially evident by part-time students who may only have contact with part-time faculty because they are employed elsewhere during daytime classes that are generally taught by full-timers.

How many students does the part-timer teach per course or per term? Often part-timers teach large sections of introductory courses, and extra students create extra work for part-time faculty.

What introductory or advanced level courses are taught by part-timers? Advanced classes require the part-timer to possess different instructional skills, and also greater content mastery.

What are the class hours and locations of part-timer's classes? They frequently are assigned class times and locations that are undesirable to full-timers. After a full day's work, teaching a class effectively to students who also may have spent a full day at work is not an easy task. In some instances, off-campus locations may not be the best environment in which to conduct a class, but the part-timer is expected to overcome the environment with excellent instructional delivery skills.

Are part-timers willing to help the institution in times of high demand? Demand by students for specific courses may require the institution to schedule a section at the last minute or to change the location of a class to accommodate more students. Part-time faculty members are expected to be flexible in these circumstances.

The evaluation system designed for part-time faculty needs to be flexible, sensitive, and systematic. It should concentrate on the evaluation of teaching effectiveness with other factors being included as needed. The purpose and use of the evaluation system should be clearly articulated verbally and in writing to part-time faculty at the beginning of employment. Evaluative data is gathered from multiple sources and the timing of data collection should be appropriately scheduled to ensure optimal results. The results of the evaluation should be discussed with the part-timer by the mentor or department chair. The results of the evaluation system form a basis for improvement as well as for performance appraisals.

Evaluation Model

Figure 2 outlines a comprehensive evaluation model for part-time faculty. The implementation of this model begins with the selection of part-time faculty. Once selected, the part-time faculty are divided into two tracks. Track one includes those who have been recently employed in similar positions at the institution. These individuals are required to attend a session to review institutional policies, evaluation procedures, and they are made aware of available equipment or instructional media.

Track two are those who are new to the institution or who have not been employed recently. They attend a general orientation, including a detailed briefing on college policies and procedures, and a campus tour. The purpose and use of the evaluation system is explained in detail with examples of the evaluation instruments provided. Questions are encouraged. Also, at this session, part-timers are assigned and introduced to faculty mentors.

All part-time and full-time faculty are urged to attend a departmental social gathering which could come at the end of the general orientation or could be a separate occasion. It provides an opportunity for all faculty to meet and to develop relationships with their colleagues. It is important for part-timers to have some sense of belonging as a member of the department. Equally important is the opportunity for interaction between full-time and part-time faculty.

Support services are rarely available during evening hours or at off-campus locations, yet they are needed by part-time faculty. Institutions that use part-time instructors may find that the availability of support services may need to be expanded into the evening hours. An evaluation system that contains a component on instructional design skills will necessitate the provision of adequate and timely support services to part-time faculty.

Part-time instructors who are expected to be assigned duties other than classroom assignments should be made aware of these expectations and how they will be evaluated. For example, the department may schedule a series of training sessions covering such items as classroom management and test construction that will focus on needs of the part-

PART-TIME FACULTY SYSTEMATIC EVALUATION MODEL

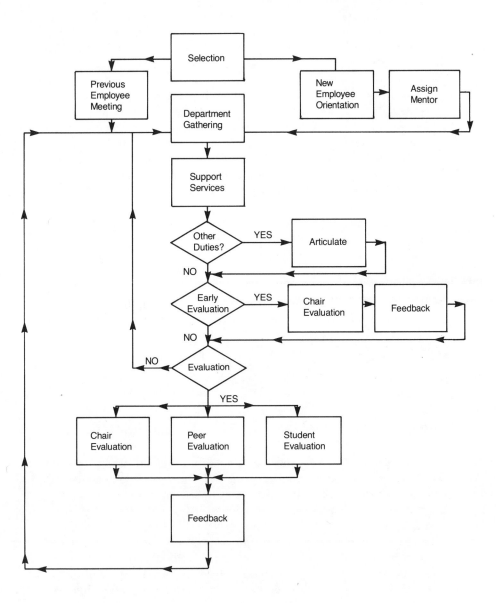

Figure 2

time faculty, or departmental policy may require the scheduling and meeting of office hours for part-time faculty.

The department chair may want to schedule a classroom visit to some classrooms early in the term. This observation may indicate areas that need immediate improvement; a faculty mentor can be called upon to assist with these problems. Individually scheduled sessions can address problems that were detected by the department chair's visitation.

All part-time faculty should be evaluated on a regular schedule, using multiple sources of evaluation data. Chair evaluations, including a classroom visit or review of a videotaped session, provide information on classroom delivery skills; student evaluations will provide information on the teacher's ability to create an effective classroom learning environment. A review of the part-timer's syllabi, class handouts, case studies, project descriptions, and other materials could provide information on content mastery as well as instructional design skills. Evaluations that are conducted on a regular schedule do not need to be completed every term for each faculty member.

The results of any evaluation are discussed with the faculty member. Each institution develops standards of performance for each category of part-time faculty, and individual performances are measured against these standards. Since each teacher has different skills, different expectations, makes unique contributions, and teaches for different reasons, flexible evaluation systems and diverse standards of performance are needed.

Summary

It is likely that the numbers of part-time faculty will continue to increase slowly, although each institution needs to have a percentage that fits its situation. Non-policy or a floating pragmatism may provide short-term gains and long-term problems. The economic benefits and flexibility made available by using part-time faculty can be crucial to institutional efficiency and effectiveness, if properly considered and used.

Sound evaluation systems, based upon proven measurements, should be in place for all part-time faculty. They should focus on teaching effectiveness yet other contributions made by part-timers cannot be ignored. In designing flexible evaluation systems, careful attention should be paid to constitutional rights and to due process.

With the many elements and factors that must be considered in developing an evaluation system, Miller offers the following insight. "We need to keep in perspective what evaluation is all about. It really is to serve students through providing better teaching and learning in a unique societal institution known as a college or university" (1986, p. 167). This perspective also describes the reason for the existence of two-year colleges.

The two-year college, as we know it today, cannot survive without part-time faculty. As part-time faculty often are teaching a sizable portion of the student body, it is imperative that evaluation systems to appraise their performances be fair and comprehensive. An integrated evaluation system is one way to provide this needed data for both formative and summative evaluation.

5

Evaluating Academic Program Effectiveness

By Charles E. Finley, J. Dennis Hart
and Mary-Louise Holloway

The demand for accountability in higher education from the student-consumer as well as from state legislatures has heightened the necessity for program review and evaluation. Legislators and funding bodies want to realize a return on their investment, and the emphasis has shifted from quantity to quality.

Although many colleges and universities have used some type of program evaluation for years, the degree to which it was formal and systematized varies among institutions. In a survey of 1,082 colleges and universities by Barak (1982), 82 percent indicated they used some type of formal program review, which was a 70 percent increase in the number of colleges engaging in program evaluation since an earlier study in 1965. Barak's research also found that two- and four-year public institutions were more likely to undertake program review and evaluation if it was required or encouraged by senior administration.

The evaluation of academic program performance serves many purposes, with a foremost reason being to improve academic programs. The evaluation allows faculty and administration to know to what extent the program is accomplishing its objectives and where alterations are needed. Program evaluation can appraise changes in students from entry to exit—the "value-added" concept. It assists administrative decision-making by providing data that can assist in determining whether a program should be maintained, modified, discontinued, or whether a new program should be initiated. Program evaluation provides a link between planning and budgeting and helps an institution make more efficient and effective use of its resources. It can be used as a basis for interdepartmental comparisons of content and quality. As part of an institution's overall evaluation process, program evaluation helps to identify how well the college is meeting its mission and goals.

Issues in Program Evaluation

The use of program review has enjoyed considerable growth in the last 10 years. Institutions of higher education, influenced by recent Blue Ribbon panels on higher education, prodded by state higher education boards, persuaded by the institution's board of trustees, and forced by the economic conditions facing higher education, are establishing systems for regular, systematic performance evaluation of their academic programs.

Myths

Along with this growth have come a number of myths regarding the use of program performance evaluation. Barak (1986) has identified several myths which have developed during the meteoric rise of program review. One common myth is that an institution does not need a program review process if the academic programs are accredited by either a regional accrediting body or a specialized accrediting group such as the National League for Nursing. While program review and accreditation outcomes both can serve legitimate purposes, they are complementary. Recommendations from accrediting bodies now encourage the use of an on-going systematic review process to establish accountability for its academic programs. The local program review process should go beyond meeting the minimum standards established by accrediting bodies and should be used to cover areas that are not addressed by accrediting bodies.

A second common myth identified by Barak is that there is only one way to do program review. A successful program review process at a large research oriented university may not be the panacea at a state-supported two-year technical college. Imitation may not be the most sincere form of flattery when it results in a review process which alienates those responsible for its implementation. The most successful program review systems are those that are developed to meet the needs and objectives of a particular institution.

A cited rationale for undertaking program review is to save money. If the primary objective of the program review is to decide the fate of a certain academic program, then savings may result. However, without taking into account both the costs and the benefits of the review process, needless time and effort may be spent in a wheel-spinning activity of major proportions. Other reviews are undertaken for the purpose of program improvement. In some cases the results may indicate a need for resource infusions to promote the excellence of these programs. Barak points out that it may be more useful to think in terms of efficiencies rather than savings as funds are reallocated to academic programs having a higher priority.

Institutions should be careful not to expect too much from the outcomes of program review. The myth that program review will produce spectacular results has gained a measure of support. Rather than providing all of the answers to the burning questions, the process may uncover new problems that need to be considered. The review process will most likely result in minor changes for the vast majority of academic programs, and these changes may take several years to implement.

Emphasis on Quality

The matter of quality is the issue that now draws greater interest in program evaluations than a few years ago. Unfortunately, funding sources do not always encourage quality in instructional programs. State funding models tend to be dysfunctional to the extent that they encourage an emphasis on the generation of full-time equivalencies (FTE) instead of program substance. Funding from federal and private sources, according to Bisesi (1984), tends to favor short-run outcomes, which also may distract faculty from efforts in instructional improvement.

Quality assurance also is a major concern of regional accrediting agencies. Troutt (1979) reviewed the standards of the six regional accreditation agencies and found that they have quality concerns about institutional purposes and objectives, educational programs, financial resources, faculty, and support services. His findings indicate that assurance of quality is often inferential. Additionally, it was found that quality was defined in a relative manner, and that any common measure of quality would destroy institutional diversity. Nonetheless, Troutt contends that quality can be measured by analyzing cognitive outcomes, contrasting information from other institutions, and student changes from matriculation to graduation.

Postsecondary institutions possess neither the time nor the human and financial resources necessary to perform annual in-depth evaluations of the institution's academic programs. To offset these limitations, an institution needs a systematic process to identify a timetable to determine when a program should be evaluated. Two approaches to scheduling of program reviews have been employed with varying success. The first approach is similar to the game of darts. Decisions concerning which programs and when to evaluate are subject to the accuracy of the person(s) responsible for program evaluation. In the hands of unimaginative persons the process encompasses more luck than skill, and valuable time and resources may be wasted. In the second approach, referred to as the "dragnet" approach, all of an institution's academic programs are rounded up and become the focus of extensive program evaluation in a single or multiple years, regardless of the need for such evaluations.

A third approach takes into account the importance attached to evaluative criteria developed by the institution, and it objectively evaluates academic programs based upon their need for evaluation. In this program review model, developed by Baratta (1976), criteria previously used by state and local administrators are used as the basis for the model. From this list the criterion are defined in quantifiable terms. The criteria are then rank-ordered and subjected to statistical evaluation using normalized T-scores. The resulting analysis provides a rank ordering by need for evaluation. The model was tested at Moraine Valley Community College and was found to be completely reliable—the only errors that occurred were error input by the data collectors. In sum, this offers a meaningful model for determining which programs need evaluation. The timing of the evaluation is left to the knowledge and discretion of the program administrator.

Program Review Models

Central to the issue of evaluating the performance of an institution's academic programs is the selection of a process to conduct the needed evaluations. Several models exist for this evaluation. The selection of a particular process should not be based upon the ease of its implementation but rather on the needs and resources of the institution. Institutions should use caution if tempted to adopt a particular model in its entirety. A better approach would be to pick and choose from components in several models depending on individual evaluation needs; in other words, adapt not adopt.

The following program review models are offered as examples from which elements may be taken and applied as needed. The first two models represent existing review processes which have found application in both four-year and two-year colleges. The third model addresses the quality issue in program evaluation.

Quantitative Measures Model

Educational programs are evaluated at the local level to determine program effectiveness and to meet state requirements concerning a program's cost-effectiveness. Additionally, professional societies require programs to document their effectiveness to retain accreditation status. A number of quantitative criteria are offered as examples of how statistical analysis can be used to address program effectiveness.

Program retention of students. Student retention is one means of measuring a program's interest in, and efforts toward, encouraging students to remain enrolled in the particular program. Percentage increases or decreases are compared with institutional standards or rates of similar institutions offering this program.

Program FTE (full-time equivalency) Count/Headcount. It is important to examine the historical trend line of FTE generation to determine whether growth, stability, or decline is evident. A headcount of students who have affiliated themselves with a particular program will also provide a measure of viability. Analyzing the trends in both measures should also be explored. Particularly useful are data trend lines over the past three-to-five years, depending upon historical availability of hard data.

Attraction of new students. To remain viable a program must demonstrate the ability to attract new students. By tracking the historical trend line of new student attraction, percentage increases and decreases can be compared against a standard of 1.00.

Training-related placement. The goal of almost all academic programs is to provide students with employment related knowledge and skills. One of the most effective measures of attaining this goal is the rate at which graduates of academic programs who seek employment are able to find it. Calculated placement rates are compared with standards set by the institution.

Number of degrees awarded. Program enrollments which are stable or increasing will be reflected eventually as an increased or stabilized rate of degrees awarded. By examining the historical trend over a three to five year period, increases or decreases can be calculated and monitored for further action. A standard should be used for appraising each three to five year period.

Average unit cost of the program. If financial data are available concerning the yearly direct cost for each program, this cost can be divided by the number of FTE enrolled in each program. These data can then be assembled as part of a trend line analysis to pinpoint shifts of the average cost of the program, and shifts can be studied in depth to determine the factors responsible.

Outcomes-Related Model

Are they learning anything in college? (Turnbull 1985) Outcomes, the results of education, have become one of the most topical ways of determining the quality of academic programs. Exit standards speak to quality (Temple 1986). The notion of evaluating outcomes is not new, as indicated by the following quotation from the 1939 American Council on Education conference:

> There was considerable discussion of the possibility of measuring the product of an institution, namely the competence of its graduates rather than its more tangible features . . . Several agencies described their experiences with measuring devices of this sort. It was agreed that all attempts to evaluate student performance should be studied and the results distributed to the membership of agencies represented at the conference.

Until recently, outcomes evaluation was seldom used because "few institutions could present any substantial evidence about the achievement of their objectives or about the quality of their graduates" (Petersen 1981). Kirkwood (1981) laments the absence of outcomes evaluation: "Unfortunately, on most campuses, assessing outcomes has not been tried and found difficult; rather it has been found difficult and seldom tried. A principal deterrent has been the lack of information about how such assessment can be accomplished." Some of the difficulties in evaluating outcomes are that it is hard to sort out causes and effects and some of the most significant outcomes are difficult to identify and measure objectively (Bowen 1974).

Nevertheless, strong pressures for outcomes evaluation are being exerted from three fronts. First, there is the academic community seeking to improve the quality of education. Then, there is the private sector expecting more uniformly high quality in the graduates they employ. Finally, there are the state legislators looking at the return from their investment in higher education (Alexander and Stark 1986).

How, then, does one go about evaluating outcomes of an academic program? One approach provides a rational, systematic basis for recommending changes in objectives, activities, and/or resources in an effort to improve the program; provides a positive environment for faculty to observe the results of their effort; and provides for direct participation by faculty which encourages a more active commitment to evaluation and the program. The following step-by-step approach is adapted from the USHER Redesign Model (McFadden 1975).

- Review the program objectives.
- Identify the outcomes or competencies expected of students at the completion of their program. These need to be identified up front and stated clearly.
- Delineate the purpose and scope of the evaluation.
- State the criteria (or standards of performance or indicators) to be used. These should be realistic, observable, and linked to the program objectives.
- Identify what will be the sources of data. They might include students, faculty, employers. Some data may already be available from the Office for Institutional Research.
- Determine the means for collection of the data. Some means are test-retest, survey, and/or quantitative measures.
- Describe how the data will be organized for evaluation analysis. The results should provide a maximum amount of useful information to both faculty and administrators.
- Identify who will conduct the evaluation. It is generally agreed that faculty are key figures.
- Set a time frame for the evaluation.
- List all the appropriate personnel who should receive copies of the results of the evaluation.
- Make decisions on the basis of the results.

Using this framework both qualitative and quantitative data can be accommodated for maximum usefulness in both administrative and academic decision-making. Ewell (1983) encourages the use of multiple indicators to enable data to be used comparatively. This approach helps to identify relative strengths and weaknesses of a program.

At the National Center for Research to Improve Postsecondary Teaching and Learning (NCRIPTAL) a whole person approach to college student outcomes has been developed. The framework consists of three areas of student growth in college—personal, social, and academic, and three forms of demonstrated change—cognitive, motivational, and behavioral. NCRIPTAL's research program is focusing on the academic arena—on outcome measures which can be related directly to classroom and program educational experiences, as illustrated in Figure 3. Outcomes evaluation data can be used in the preparation of accreditation

Figure 3.

NCRIPTAL's Outcome Framework

Form of Measurement	Academic Arena
Cognitive	Achievement (facts, principles, ideas, skills)
	Critical-thinking skills
	Problem-solving skills
Motivational	Satisfaction with college
	Involvement/effort
	Motivation
	Self-efficacy
Behavioral	Career and life goal exploration
	Exploration of diversity
	Persistence
	Relationships with faculty

From: *Focusing on Student Academic Outcomes* by Joanne M. Alexander and Joan S. Stark, 1986. Copyright 1986 by The Regent of the University of Michigan.

self-studies, for academic program review, in institutional planning and budget review activities, in developing student retention strategies, and in developing recruitment materials and strategies (Ewell 1983).

Integrated Feedback Model

When an academic program is initially considered for adoption, the institution brings together a broad range of expertise to examine the proposal. Often included in the process are state agencies, local leaders from business and industry, outside accrediting agencies, faculty committees, and consultants. A wide range of input facilitates prudent and thorough evaluation of the proposed curriculum. This diversity of expertise can bring similar success to the process of evaluating current programs as well. This broad range of perspectives is especially valuable when the evaluation is based on identifying program quality. Such an approach usually involves at least some non-quantifiable information, and, as Seitz (1981) and others have pointed out the inherent usefulness of non-quantifiable information, it is made more valuable when a balance of viewpoints can keep information in perspective. Therefore, for schools interested in incorporating the recent concern for quality into their program evaluation, integrating feedback from numerous sources can generate an appropriate model.

Using student input. A. Astin (1982) advocates an approach to program assessment that is based upon quality measurement and a broad range of perspectives. He observes that one group that can bring a valuable perspective to the assessment process is the current student body. Students can point out possible drawbacks to a curriculum's course sequencing, the utilization of lab equipment in coursework, the textbook's usefulness, and a program's advising system. Also suggested is the periodic surveying of how students spend their time outside of class. Astin suggests that because time-on-task theories say that how students spend their time has a direct effect on how much and what they learn, such data could be useful and could be gathered through relatively inexpensive surveys. Data on how much they study and how they interact with each other and with faculty members—can provide insight into an academic program. Astin concludes that a student-oriented approach to planning and evaluation implies that the institution knows how its programs are perceived and how they are impacting its students.

Raulf and Ayres (1987) reinforce Astin's point that students are the consumers of a school's programs and that their input should be considered carefully. They stress that student feedback should be sought each term on matters of course content, delivery systems, and relevance. Too often student feedback is restricted to the process of faculty evaluation, rather than solicited for the program at large. It is acknowledged that many schools do not consider student feedback to be sufficiently valid for incorporation into formal program evaluation. In these instances, student feedback can be used as an early warning system to identify programs that may warrant a formal assessment.

Using advisory committees. For community colleges that offer occupational programs, a primary concern is relevancy. In this regard, a necessary component in the evaluation procedure is a perspective that is external to the institution, and one such source is the program advisory committee. Ertel (1980) observes that apprehension still exists regarding reliance on input from sources outside the academic environment; however, he also stresses that through the proper use of an advisory committee, program limitations and needs can be addressed expeditiously. Garrity (1984) suggests that appropriate tasks for committees include reviewing program objectives, course requirements, and course content. All these efforts lead to program relevance.

Maximum benefits are derived from advisory committees that are provided with (1) a set of guidelines, (2) clarity in program objectives, and (3) a direction of purpose (Ertel 1980). Schools that offer appropriate guidance have found the unique expertise offered by advisory committees to be vital in developing and maintaining high quality programs. Hagerstown, Maryland Junior College, for example, involves its advisory committees in program evaluation as a primary function.

Experience indicates that schools should be prepared for differences in perspective when involving employers in program evaluation. Rislov (1979) notes that the community college should be willing to understand the employers' view of educational needs; for example, from their perspective a curriculum's general education courses may not have much relevancy. And for community colleges' non-occupational programs, advisory committees can have a meaningful role in program evaluation. Outside expertise can be sought from faculty members from regional four-year colleges and universities where program graduates commonly transfer upon graduation.

A plan for meshing input from both internal and external perspectives was outlined by Gill and Nolan (1981); it was used at Hillsborough Community College (Florida), Sumter Technical College (South Carolina), and Brevard Community College (Florida). This approach begins with departmental faculty members working with colleagues who teach that program's support courses, with students, and with advisory committee members to develop 10-12 exit competencies for graduates. These competencies form the basis of questionnaires that are sent to graduates, graduates' employers, and professors at regional four-year schools that regularly receive graduates. These instruments ask (a) to what degree are these competencies needed, and (b) how well were they taught? The value of this model at integrating internal and external input is evidenced by adaptations of it being implemented in two-year colleges in Ohio, Illinois, and Kansas as well as the states already mentioned.

Still another resource for integrated feedback is the institution's own curriculum committee, which is too often restricted to evaluating programs under consideration for adoption. An interdepartmental perspective can be equally worthwhile in evaluating on-going programs. Raulf and Ayres (1987) suggest that new programs be examined two-years after initiation to assess if objectives are being met. Thereafter, they suggest a five-year cycle for evaluation.

Still another approach to integrating feedback was developed at the University of Nebraska where multiple perspectives were sought in identifying "areas of excellence" within the institution to receive special state funding. Braskamp (1982) explains that committees were formed for each area of excellence; they included faculty members who were internal and external to the institution, an academic administrator, a student, a regent, a state legislator, and a representative of the governor's office. For a three-year period, committees made annual visits, reviewed departmental self-studies, and reviewed goals and progress toward them. At the end of the three-year period, committees had developed a vehicle for assessing quality that could be used by a campus-wide review committee composed of faculty members who were internal and external to the university, alumni, and students. A primary task of the team is the ongoing assessment of program quality.

Although a variety of combinations have been examined, the common theme revolves around an institution's recognition that assessment of program quality is a task best accomplished when a range of perspectives are coordinated to create a balance and to assure a high degree of thoroughness. The model in Figure 4 indicates the range of viewpoints available to administrators wishing to overlook no valuable perspectives in pursuit of program quality.

Criteria for Successful Program Evaluation

This chapter now outlines concerns for accountability that have spurred an increased interest in program evaluation in two-year colleges, and several approaches or models have been mentioned. Although the approaches employed by institutions vary greatly, some fundamental principles are common among those that are the most effective. Seitz (1981) observes that successful evaluations are systematic because only in this way can a program's relative strengths and weaknesses be adequately measured. To facilitate a systematic evaluation, he offers the following basic steps:

1. Define the scope.
2. Specify inputs, activities, and outputs.
3. Determine the types of data to be compiled.
4. Identify the support services and personnel to be involved in the evaluation.
5. Schedule, carefully and consistently.
6. Collect and compile data.
7. Compare, critique, and analyze.
8. Draw conclusions.

Arns and Poland (1980) observe other commonalities among successful program evaluations. First, they have no single fixed protocol. They are flexible enough to realize that no two academic programs are alike. Second, the review process includes not only those persons within the program, but also those who are responsible for it such as the dean or

INTEGRATED FEEDBACK
MODEL

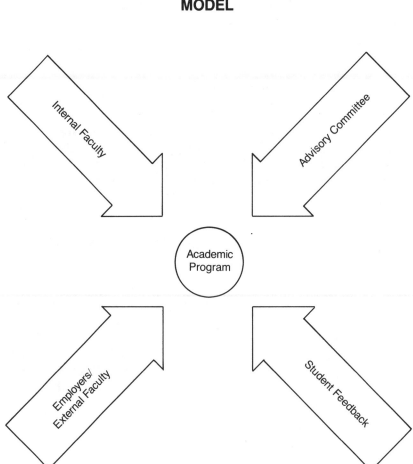

Figure 4

chief academic officer. They also stress the value of a self-study component, peer coordination, external review, and an atmosphere of openness.

Focusing on program evaluation at community colleges, Clowes (1981) offers the following six criteria for successful assessments, regardless of the model employed: (1) clear goals; (2) congruent activities; (3) satisfactory horizontal and vertical mobility for student transfer; (4) a thread of unity whether it be social, cultural, or economic; (5) effective personnel utilization including part-time faculty; and (6) cost effectiveness. These criteria can provide a framework that offers confidence in the process regardless of the model employed, and in the ability of the model to generate an appraisal worthy of the institutional investment.

6

Evaluating Student Services Programs

By Deborah Kladivko and Stephen Rostek

S tudent services programs have long played a very important role in two-year college life. Simply stated, the role of student services is to help students develop both personally and educationally, and to help them work their way through the obstacles that they face during their college careers. The functions normally incorporated under the student services title include admissions, financial aid, registration and records, student activities, career planning and placement, counseling, orientation, and academic advising.

Student services programs can be grouped into two categories: general and specific. *General* programs are common to most institutions and serve a large portion of the student body, such as the entire admissions function at an institution. *Specific* programs or activities are incorporated under these more general programs and serve a special target group or perform a special function, such as a Minority Recruitment Day program, or a college day program for high school students.

Student services programs are especially important at the two-year college level because of the many different types of students. This diverse group brings with it many different problems and needs that should be addressed by the student services area. McDaniel and Lombardi (1972, p. 81) stated that the "compelling purpose of student . . . services is the individualizing of the total impact of the college community upon each individual student." At two-year colleges the individualization of programs and services is critical to assuring student success.

Evaluations of student services programs are conducted to determine the merit and worth of each program. In the past, many student services evaluations were based on hunches or impressions (Kuh 1979), on tradition (Crabbs and Crabbs 1978, p. 41), or on idealistic and humanitarian grounds rather than on tangible evidence of results (Harpel 1976, p. ii). However, as the demand for accountability in colleges became greater, so did the need for a more systematic method for evaluating student services programs.

Methods of structuring the evaluation process for student service programs do not differ significantly from basic evaluation in other areas. Payne (1974) presented a five-step model for program evaluation that can be applied to the evaluation of student services programs: (1) identify specific detailed goals and objectives, (2) design the evaluation system, (3) select measures and data-gathering methods, (4) collect the data, and (5) analyze, interpret, report, and apply the useful statistics.

The first three steps in Payne's model are the most important and the most complex. This chapter will be devoted to an examination of these three steps as they relate to the student services area. To this end, the why, what, how, who, and when questions of student services evaluation will be addressed. The "why" question deals with the purposes of evaluation, the "what" with the criteria to be used, the "how" with the methodology available, the "who" with the choice of evaluators, and the "when" with the timing of evaluation.

Why: Purposes of Evaluation

The first step in planning an effective evaluation is determining its specific and general purposes. Why is the evaluation being conducted and for whom? What uses will be made of the information generated by the evaluation? Once the purposes have been identified, they will serve as the rudder that will steer the rest of the evaluation process. Purposes commonly associated with evaluations of student services programs include:

Generating feedback to improve programs. Many evaluations are conducted to generate information that will help the programmer to improve the program. Future students benefit from the feedback provided by program participants. Improvement is often the goal of evaluations of *general* student services programs.

Determining whether a program should be continued or abolished.

Evaluating a program to determine its effectiveness provides the decision-maker with information that will help him or her determine whether continued time and effort should be put into the program. This information becomes increasingly important as resources become more limited and decision-makers are forced into the position of reallocating scarce resources. Evaluations of *specific* student services programs, such as special events or activities, are commonly conducted for this purpose.

Identifying unmet needs. No student services program can meet all the needs of all students. Evaluating existing programs often leads to the identification of unmet needs. If particular unmet needs are mentioned often, then the student services professional can attempt to meet these needs with additional programming.

Gathering evidence to justify increased staffing or resources. It is unlikely that any student services operation will secure increased staffing or resources without providing strong evidence that indicates (a) that a need for this increase exists, and (b) that current resources are being put to good use. The proper use of evaluation can provide evidence in both of these areas.

What: Criteria

After the purposes of an evaluation have been determined, criteria upon which to base the evaluation can be chosen. The determination of adequate criteria is one of the most persistent and challenging problems involved in the evaluation of student services programs because of the nature of the programs. (Fordyce 1972). For example, the evaluation of a student activities program at a large urban two-year college should not be based on the same criteria as the evaluation of the student activities at a small residential college. Kauffman (1984, p. 29) writes that it is important "to use criteria and standards appropriate to the mission and goals of individual institutions."

When choosing criteria to be used in an evaluation, it is important to keep in mind the basic question, "What do I really want to know?" In many cases more than one criterion needs to be applied in order to generate the proper information. Eight criteria (Fordyce 1972; Kauffman 1984; Kuh 1979) on which many student services evaluations are based include:

Quantity and frequency. The number of students who use a particular program or service and the frequency of use are taken by many student services professionals as measures of the popularity of or need for the program. Information about the quantity and frequency of use is usually easy to obtain; however, one limitation of this criterion is that numbers alone may not be an accurate indicator of the program's worth. Programs designed for special needs groups, such as minority students or battered women, will attract fewer students than programs designed for the entire student body. This criterion should be used in combination with other measures.

Satisfaction level. The degree to which students are satisfied with a program is often used as an indicator of the worth of a program. Kauffman (1984), however, points out the limitations of using satisfaction level as the sole measure of the worth of the program. He states that although dissatisfaction with a program probably indicates that the program is ineffective in some respect, satisfaction with a program does not necessarily mean that it is educationally beneficial.

Scope. The scope of both general and specific student services programs can be evaluated, and determining the scope of a program involves evaluating whether all important areas are covered. A general financial aid program might be determined to have too narrow a scope if no achievement-based scholarships were available to its students. A specific Financial Aid Information Night might be considered to have too narrow a scope if the presentation lacked information about how to apply for loans.

Scope is an appropriate criterion for evaluating a program if the purpose of the evaluation is to determine unmet needs. For the other purposes presented in this paper, however, it would most likely be best if scope was used in conjunction with several other criteria for determining the worth of a program.

Awareness level and reputation. A program cannot be successful unless the constituencies for which it is designed are aware that the program exists; therefore, the measure of awareness levels can indicate much about the potential success or failure of a program. In addition to being aware of a program, the reputation of the program also contributes to the success or failure of a program. For example, if the counseling center is viewed as being only for those who cannot handle their problems on their own, students who need help may be discouraged from making use of the resources provided by the center. If, on the other hand, the counseling center is seen as a place where students can receive valuable help during times of stress, they may feel comfortable taking advantage of these services.

Cost effectiveness. Although many student services programs are based on humanistic and student development principles, the reality of financial constraints must also be considered. Evaluation on the basis of cost effectiveness is especially important during times of limited resources. Cost effectiveness can be defined in many ways. The amount of staff time devoted per student involved and the total dollars spent on a program are but two of these ways. As mentioned earlier, pure numbers do not adequately represent the value of a program. The perceived value to a student should also be considered when a program is evaluated on the basis of cost effectiveness.

Goal achievement. Whenever a program is planned with a particular goal in mind, it can be evaluated by the extent to which it achieved the intended goal. Management-by-objectives is an example of a system which evaluates on the basis of goal achievement. Although goal achievement can be an appropriate criterion for evaluation, this criterion does not indicate whether the original goal was appropriate or not; it simply measures the extent to which the goal was achieved. Consequently, this criterion also should be used in conjunction with other criteria.

Outcomes. Using the outcomes criterion involves determining the changes that occurred in students because of a particular program. Determining short-term outcomes of specific programs, such as determining the amount of factual knowledge gained by students from an AIDS Awareness seminar, can be accomplished rather easily; measuring long-term and less quantifiable outcomes of specific programs, such as evaluating the effect of the AIDS program on sexual values and attitudes, can be quite difficult. Determining the outcomes of a general program, such as the development of leadership potential caused by involvement in the student activities program, is also difficult because students are exposed to many different influences and it is difficult to identify what factors actually affected the change in the student behavior.

Contribution to institutional missions and goals. An effective institution is not comprised of many different factions working towards their own ends; rather, it is a whole which is made up of parts that support the functioning and goals of the whole. The goals of student services should be designed to contribute to the missions and goals of the institution; therefore, one criterion upon which to base student services evaluations is the extent to which the program contributes to larger educational missions. For example, a career planning program should contribute to an institutional goal of providing for the vocational development of students; and providing a remedial education program can be linked to the institutional goal of providing postsecondary educational opportunities for diverse populations.

Evaluating programs in terms of contribution to institutional goals and mission, although challenging, not only provides valuable information about the worth of a program, but also lends credibility to and justification for programs that are found to be supportive of these larger goals.

How: Method of Evaluation

Once the criteria have been identified, the next, and critical, step is determining the method to be used for systematically gathering data for the evaluation. Care needs to be taken to consider both the criteria that the evaluation should address and the possible obstacles that might hinder that evaluation. The obstacles associated with student services program evaluations that can serve to limit the choice of a method for gathering data (Crabbs and Crabbs 1978; Fordyce 1972) include:

Subjectivity of information. Many student services programs deal with student development issues, which, because of their nature, are not easily quantifiable. For example, determining the amount of self-awareness that a student gained through a student services program would be difficult to measure with traditional methods because many of these methods deal only with quantifiable data. The evaluator is faced with the task of either finding a way to quantify "self-awareness," or choosing a research method that is designed for subjective information.

Interrelated factors. As mentioned earlier, a student's growth and development is influenced by many different factors, among which are student services programs. Because of the interrelatedness of these factors, it is sometimes difficult to identify the actual contribution that a specific student services program made to this overall development; therefore, evaluators need to make special efforts to choose evaluation methods that are best able to analyze interrelated factors.

Lack of normative data. Because of the situational nature of student services programs, little normative data exist on student services program evaluations; therefore, the process of comparing evaluations of a particular program to state or national standards, which is a common evaluation technique in many areas, has its limitations when applied to the student services area. Although these obstacles can serve to limit the types of evaluation methods that are appropriate in a given situation, they should not be used as reasons for not conducting evaluations, rather, they should be considered along with other criteria when choosing an evaluation method.

The tools for gathering information can vary from informal and simplistic to rigidly structured and complex. If only an informal review of a seminar on resume writing is desired, then a short questionnaire at the end of the presentation can obtain the perceptions of participants as to the value of the seminar and its contents. If, however, an intercollegiate sports program at a two-year institution is being reviewed for possible discontinuation, a much more complex mechanism is needed. More complex and subjective issues, such as referral counseling processes or initial placement testing procedures, may require several tools to obtain the information for a total picture of the operation.

The key to the completion of a successful evaluation process is matching the criteria with an appropriate strategy or method for collecting selected data. Crabbs and Crabbs (1978, p. 44) list 10 possible strategies for the evaluation of the counseling setting in student services: (1) satisfaction surveys, (2) experimental design, (3) status studies, (4) tabulation, (5) follow-up and outcome, (6) case study, (7) achievement of goals, (8) time cost analysis, (9) ecological perspectives, and (10) model/function.

As can be seen when the criteria from the previous section are compared to these strategies, matching criteria and strategies is possible. For example, satisfaction surveys can be useful in obtaining client opinions or satisfaction levels; tabulation can be used to generate data on numbers of students using services and the frequency with which these services are used; cost effectiveness can utilize cost-benefit analysis; and the follow-up and outcome and achievement of goals methods can be directly matched with outcomes and achievement of goals criteria. It is important in this matching process that evaluation in the student services area should be program specific. Each program evaluation should be based on the purpose for the evaluation and on the specific criteria identified as important in that program.

Non-quantified methods. The quantifiability of data is a major factor to be considered when matching criteria with methods; however, since student service programs are student interaction intensive, much of what transpires within any given program may not be quantifiable. Brown (1978, p. 124) identified three methods of program evaluation that emphasize observed interaction rather than numerical quantification or consumer perception. A "goal-free" process is one in which the evaluator is unaware of the structured goals as developed by the staff. The objective is to observe the program, identify the outcomes, compare observed to planned outcomes, and to use these data to evaluate not only the program but the planning process as well. The added value to this method is that it may uncover outcomes unanticipated by the deliverers.

A "responsive" approach to assessment would be to *not* zero in on outcomes, just to document the events of the program, and record the actual versus the intended transactions. In this way, the evaluator could respond to the need for information while valuing the perspective of the consumer.

A third approach would be "transactional," in which the program would be viewed as a change process. As change occurs, so will conflict. Part of the evaluator's role in this approach is to rechannel energies for positive results, diagnosing as well as assessing the system for improvement. Each of these three approaches to evaluation emphasizes observation and interaction rather than compilation of numbers and perceptions. The value of these types of approaches is summarized by Goodrich (1978, p. 631), who warns against the pursuit of objectivity: "We limit ourselves to what we think we can measure well and so often focus on the trivial parts of the program."

Quantified approaches. A more quantifiable approach was offered by Stufflebeam and others (1971) in the Context-Input-Process-Product (CIPP) Model, in which the four areas denoted in the title are analyzed individually and then together for the entire program, and an evaluative conclusion is then reached.

Surveys and tabulations are two other methods commonly used to obtain quantifiable information. The survey is the most common means for soliciting information, and it can be as simple as a verbal "did you enjoy the program?" or as complex as a multi-page document asking a multitude of questions. A Likert scale could be attached to subjective questions to add "quantifiability" to the results. In addition, different constituent groups can be surveyed and their various perceptions compared.

Simple tabulations involve documenting program information such as number of participants, frequency of use, dollars expended, and hours of preparation time required. Tabulated data may be difficult to evaluate because of the lack of normative data; therefore, longitudinal comparisons from year-to-year may be more useful. An up-front commitment to offer a program two or three times to obtain comparable data lends more credibility to the evaluative process than the discontinuation after running the program only once and having no basis for comparisons. In internal longitudinal studies, the institution determines the level of acceptability of the program results.

From the variety of approaches reviewed here, it can be seen that matching the criteria of evaluation to the appropriate method may not be an easy task. In addition, obstacles to evaluation need to be considered. The magnitude of the program and its resulting evaluation, budget impact, and interrelatedness to other programs also play important roles in the selection and success of program evaluation. Each of these approaches has merit relative to the evaluation of a particular program. An additional decision that needs to be given consideration at the time of method selection is the choice of evaluator(s).

Who: The Evaluator(s)

There are basically two types of evaluators: Those who are conducting the evaluation (recorders or assessors), and those who provide input to the program that is being assessed, such as clients, deliverers, and supervisors. In some cases, the assessors may also be the deliverers.

The term "evaluator" is most commonly applied to those persons whose input is desired in an effort to evaluate a program. A wide range of groups may be solicited for input, and Ford (1979) points out the need for information from five groups in program evaluation: potential users, those who manage the program, those knowledgeable about institutional policies and procedures, those with political influence on campus and faculty, and those with technical skills in the program area. These categories may overlap and input from all categories may not be necessary, but consideration should be given to each group as a potential source of information.

Evaluators are chosen on the basis of the purpose of the evaluation, the scope of the program, the methods to be used, and budgetary considerations. When the purpose of the evaluation is to improve programs or to identify unmet needs, the programmer commonly serves as the assessor, soliciting input from the students who take part in the program. This pattern often is used in specific programs with narrow scope such as those in a one-day workshop format where an exit questionnaire is administered by those conducting the event to determine its usefulness. Another similar situation is when an informal review is indicated. There is much less pressure for structure in or formal validation of the data-gathering mechanism in this situation. Given this perspective, little objection would be expected to permitting the program delivery team or one of its members to collect the evaluation data.

On the other hand, when the program being reviewed has major impact because of its scope or budgetary size or when the evaluation will have major impact because of its purpose, which may be to continue or abolish the program or to justify additional staffing or resources, care needs to be taken in the selection of the evaluators. Evaluators should be chosen from pertinent constituencies. If, for example, an intercollegiate sports program is being reviewed for possible discontinuation, four major constituencies should be consulted for input: the players, the fans (student body, faculty members, other employees), the community (to determine the potential economic impact of the decision), and the college staff members most able to assess the public relations value of the program as a recruiting asset.

Although potential conflict of interest should be considered when selecting assessors for any evaluation, it is especially important in cases where the evaluation will have major impact. In these cases, the assessors normally should not be part of the program delivery team. Not only those close to the program but also those distanced from it but vying for the same funding dollars should be relieved of the possible pressure of conflict of interest. If input from these groups is desired, however, forming an evaluation committee that includes representatives from many different constituencies, including those just mentioned, may serve to neutralize possible conflict of interest.

Trembley and Sharf's (1975, p. 249) discussion of internal and external evaluation summarizes the process to this point. Internal (self) evaluation by the deliverers of a program enable them to know it in greater detail, to define its place and priority within the institution, to tabulate its functional value in daily activity, and to estimate its effect on clients, faculty, and staff. External evaluation by persons on or off campus who may be clients or observers should result in a more unbiased review of the process and outcomes of any given program.

When: Timing

The final step in the process involves the timing of the evaluation. Timing is a critical issue when quality output is expected from an assessment. There are three aspects of timing that should be considered when implementing a program evaluation. First, the processes and techniques should be structured so that an optimal amount of the desired information is obtained in a minimum of time. Consideration should be given to those persons who will be asked to complete an evaluation form or to participate in an evaluation discussion.

A second consideration is the placement of the evaluation mechanism within the program. If the purpose of the evaluation is formative, then the evaluation should be placed at strategic intervals within the progression of the program with as little disruption as possible. If the purpose is summative, it should be placed at or soon after the end of the program to solicit the most informed results. Too long of a wait after the program has finished may permit the participants to forget important information.

Finally, timeliness of response to the results of the evaluation is important. Sharing the results of the evaluation with participants (if applicable), deliverers, and administrators is crucial if the process is to be viewed as useful. Information not shared elicits suspicion and distrust and can have a negative impact on cooperation in future evaluative endeavors. The results of the evaluation should be seriously considered for the process to remain credible.

Occasionally, evaluation is conducted for less-than-noble purposes, or the process is "rigged" to produce results that someone wants, or the process is really a non-process. Speaking to evaluation avoidance/manipulation strategies, Burck and Peterson (1975) identified seven aspects of academic gamesmanship that have been used in student services program evaluation as well as elsewhere.

1. **Sample-of-One Method.** Discuss the problem with a few colleagues and arrive at consensus.

2. **Brand A versus Brand B Method.** Compare nonequivalent groups to make the program look good.

3. **Sunshine Method.** Provide evidence of program quantity through client data with no evidence of quality.

4. **Goodness-of-Fit Method.** Display how well the program fits into already established procedures.

5. **Committee Method.** A group connected to the program comes to consensus and writes a report to the administration about the program's value.

6. **Shot-in-the-Dark Method.** Search for any kind of program impact because there are no clear objectives for the program, or the evaluation is not related to them.

7. **Anointed-by-Authority Method.** Hire nationally recognized consultants to confirm predetermined results by talking to the "right people."

Characteristics of a Good Model

There are various paths that can be followed in the pursuit of program evaluation in student services. An effective model will analyze program, method, and results to answer the questions why, what, how, who, and when. Each successive step of the process builds on the previous step, culminating in the acquisition and evaluation of information pertinent to the review of the program in question.

In addition, there are some fundamental components inherent to the evaluation process that increase the probability of acquiring the desired information to the satisfaction of those involved. The first component is staff input. The deliverers should have input in the construction/selection of the assessment mechanism and its resulting support process.

Second, the process should be sufficiently flexible to permit change, if not during the process then at least after summative review. This point does not say that change should be made for the sake of change, but flexibility does provide an opportunity for adjustments.

Third, the cost/benefit ratio of the evaluation should not prohibit the evaluation. Basic cost guidelines need to be developed before the process is limited by human and material expenses. An expensive external experimental research design may be prohibitive, but an acceptable alternative normally can be found.

Finally, frequent communication is necessary, both within the evaluation group and externally with sources that are likely to be affected by possible changes. There is a fine line between not giving people enough information and inundating them with unneeded or unwanted information; therefore it is advisable to query constituents in the beginning to determine how much they wish to be involved.

Summary

In addition to following a systematic model for evaluation, there are some general dimensions to consider in the evaluation of student services programs. As new specific programs are proposed, each one should have a required evaluation component that is structured to reflect the program's value to the institution. If specific programs are changed to general programs or when general programs are reviewed for improvement, the criteria for success should be clearly outlined and shared with users, deliverers, and other concerned institutional constituents.

Recognizing that funding plays a key role in the continuation of all programs and that budgeting is significantly an institutional political process, program proponents need to sharpen their political skills to increase their chances of continued institutional support. Program deliverers need not compromise their professional and personal beliefs to obtain an ultimate goal, but it is important to know who within the institution's decision-making structure should be consulted on issues germane to program needs and who should be kept informed as to the needs and values of new programs.

Since the demand for accountability is not expected to diminish in the near future, student services personnel should increase their knowledge of evaluation processes and use this knowledge in the development of new programs and the review of existing ones. The evaluation mechanism needs to be seen as legitimate, and the more knowledge a staff member has about the evaluation process, the more legitimate the evaluation is likely to be.

An institution should strive to involve people meaningfully in the evaluation process. Active participation of institutional staff as well as clients of a program gives each group a sense of ownership of the program and is more likely to elicit an honest effort toward a fair evaluation of the program.

The results of the evaluation should be shared with the participants and a plan of action to implement the results should be part of the evaluative structure. Without this communication and legitimizing of the process, there is a strong possibility that negative attitudes will develop, not only toward the program that is being evaluated but also toward participation in future evaluations.

For evaluation to be seen as a valuable and integral component of student services programming, it should be perceived that the evaluation is legitimate, the data generated is valid, the participants are concerned about validity, the results will be used or at least seriously considered, and the process is more than a response to external pressure.

7

Evaluating Administrative Performance

By Dwight Greer and Gene Wilson

T he issue of accountability is not only an agenda item for four-year public or private institutions but for two-year colleges as well. Postsecondary educational organizations need plans for their own organizational development, and evaluation plays a major role in this evolving process. As two-year colleges continue to become more complex organizations, evaluation will become an increasingly important aspect of an institution's mission and goals.

The number of college administrators increased from one for every five faculty members to one for every four in the mid-1970s (Semas 1987, p. 7). The increasing complexity of two-year colleges requires more administrative staffing in areas such as student services, continuing education, admissions, fiscal affairs, and public affairs. Today, the administrative staff may total one-third of the professional staff at a smaller two-year institution. Due to this growth in staffing and also because it is sound personnel management practice, evaluation of administrators has become more imperative.

The current national attention to quality/excellence carries with it an increasing call for greater accountability. No longer is it the faculty that is raising the issue of evaluation for administrators, but governing boards, the public, and administrators themselves have joined in this refrain.

Rationale for Administrative Evaluation

It is an issue for fairness. Millett (1980, p. 19) wrote that "evaluation of a college or university is necessarily of two kinds: an evaluation of the people in an enterprise or an evaluation of the outcome of the enterprise. Because the university is a labor-intensive enterprise, the performance of its personnel is of critical importance." If faculty members are to be evaluated, then so should administrators who are part of the labor-intensive enterprise.

It is an issue of self-development. Administrative performance improvement comes about through experience, to be sure, but the importance of performance evaluation and professional growth opportunities are not so widely understood. Administrative evaluation is the basic building block for such self-development. Too often evaluation systems and models are concerned almost exclusively with outcomes when an equally important question is: "How do we improve performance through assessment?" Evaluation for two-year college administrators can improve performance.

It is an issue of sound personnel policy. Any organization, as it maps its growth and development, should have a route to follow, and an essential element is how efficient and effective are its leaders. What are their strengths and weaknesses? To what extent does one promote from within its ranks? Should a contract be renewed? Should disciplinary action be taken? What percentage of salary increase is equitable? Answers to these and other questions are greatly facilitated by having some form of evaluation as a basis for judgment.

It is an issue of good management. Two-year college administrators desire some sort of feedback on their job performance; good management requires evaluation as well as feedback. The primary purpose of providing feedback to the person that has been evaluated is for self-appraisal of personal performance and to set the conditions for either meaningful self-initiated or supervisor-initiated performance changes (Goodwin and Smith 1985).

It is an issue of an institution's goals, mission, and objectives. Evaluation allows for an institution to know more about where it has been and where it is heading. How does one know about performance strengths and weaknesses without some form of systematic evaluation? Wattenbarger (1983, p. 47) speaks about administrative evaluation: "An effective evaluation plan is necessary because it provides a formal framework for the individual in an organization to discuss performance, achievements, and hindrances from a personal and individual point of view and from an organizational point of view." Lahti (1975, p. 9), writing from an MBO perspective, outlines three products that come from evaluation: The institution learns or becomes aware of the individual manager's performance which provides the flow of data; the improvement and advancement of the organization itself; and information linkage to better forms of decision making.

Instituting an Evaluation Plan

The following guidelines may be useful in developing an administrative evaluation system in two-year colleges. The evaluation system should be clearly articulated, including policies and procedures and formative and summative purposes. If the administrative units are unclear of the administration's mission, it is possible that administrative duties may falter and lack direction as well as organizational cohesiveness.

The evaluation instruments and systems as well as the policies for evaluation should be approved and supported by the executive level of management. Administrative evaluation should be considered as a system, having written statements covering all phases, such as purposes, processes (at the same time each year), who sends what correspondence to whom, and possible outcomes. Administrative evaluations should be done on a regular basis—annually. And evaluation should seek also to improve internal communication.

Miller (1979, p. 181) offers these questions for appraising one's current administrative system: Have the policies and procedures for evaluating administrators been examined recently? Do these policies and procedures allow for a fair, searching, and appropriately confidential system? And are they designed finally to improve performance? Are the formal procedures carried out regularly and applied to all administrators? Are the results shown to the individual who has been evaluated, and does this person have access to an appeals procedure before any results are shared with others? Does the institution have a way to appraise the overall specific effectiveness of the evaluation process?

Turning to guidelines for establishing an effective program of evaluation for two-year college administrators, the following 10 points are based upon writings by Farmer (1979, pp. 178-180).

1. Do not start until there is sufficient time and energy. Evaluation plays an important role in two-year colleges' missions, and failure to expend the needed energy on developing an effective evaluation program can result in failure.
2. Evaluation should be rooted in the traditions and organizational

climate of each institution. Two-year colleges should *adapt not adopt* evaluation approaches to their specific institutions. Trying to copy or duplicate other evaluation programs may not be a wise decision.

3. Clarify the institution's mission and goals. The development of an organization is dependent upon individuals who are striving to reach specific personal and organizational goals and objectives.

4. Evaluation criteria and norms should be agreed upon in advance. Evaluating an administrator's performance requires some form of comparison in relationship to roles, duties, and functions. Administrators need to know in advance how they will be evaluated and with what criteria.

5. Evaluation data should be descriptive prior to being judgmental. Questions should be phrased to elicit descriptions of an administrator's performance before passing judgment.

6. Policies and procedures should be the result of participative planning. Evaluation programs should develop commitment which comes from direct involvement of individuals being evaluated as well as appropriate others.

7. Accept apparent contradictions in evaluation results. Actions by an administrator may be in the best interests of one constituency but not another.

8. Establish an appeals procedure. Everyone has the right of due process to check the validity of his or her evaluation.

9. Consider linking evaluation to the reward system. Promotion, increased wages, and positive reinforcement do motivate, but care must be taken that the reward system does not become devisive.

10. Add a developmental component. Evaluation is much more than just rating scales and MBO outlines. The question is: What is done with the evaluations? Does that information flow toward helping individuals meet the mission and goals of the institution?

Appraisal Methods

The design and structure of an evaluation tool is time consuming, complicated, and sensitive. The following appraisal procedures are adapted from Bergquist and Tenbrink (1978, pp. 1493-1498):

The unstructured narration or essay appraisal. This appraisal method has been used often in administrative evaluations. The administrator being evaluated is asked by the evaluator to write on the specific activities, responsibilities, duties, functions, and accomplishments over a specific time period.

The unstructured documentation. This form of evaluation is basically self-directed. The administrator being evaluated keeps records, data, and recommendations of all activities as they relate to job duties and functions. The structure in this approach consists of having a written agreement about what is to be included and the time period to be covered.

Structured narration. Using a survey or questionnaire, the individual being evaluated answers general questions on a number of items, such as accomplishments, performance, strengths, weaknesses, and problems.

Rating scales. This form of evaluation is widely used. To make the performance interview more meaningful, the same form can be completed by both the evaluator and the evaluated. Castetter and Heigher (1971) offer six potential problems with using rating scales: Most scales do not incorporate institutional expectations into the scheme of things; they are not 100 percent accurate in evaluating specific job responsibilities; questions and concerns about validity of rating scales can be raised; individuals may have biases that negatively impact upon evaluations; it is very difficult to capture on paper the "total" person; and the organization itself may bias the evaluator and the administrator being evaluated.

Structured documentation. The evaluator and the evaluated review the duties and functions of the administrator's responsibilities and set evaluative criteria to match position functions. This approach requires more communication as well as extensive data collection that documents performance.

Management by objectives. The MBO method of evaluation is a total appraisal system based upon goal outcomes at all levels of the organization. There is an established mission for each administrative level and for each administrator; and throughout a given year, supervisors follow the progress of subordinates as they strive toward specific goals. This form of evaluation may be the most responsive to the philosophical elements found in self-development theory. It also is the most time consuming method.

Difficulties and Concerns

Repeating what has been said for developing appraisal methods, evaluating two-year college administrators is complicated, sensitive, and not easy. For example, what impact do internal and external circumstances have in evaluating administrators? A number of elements may cause problems in evaluating administrative functions—elements such as retrenchment, employee strikes, enrollment decline, new leadership, and governmental, community, state, or local fiscal problems. The American Association of State Colleges and Universities (1976, p. 12) developed a number of cautions with respect to administrator evaluation that are applicable to two-year colleges:

- Avoid developing evaluation instruments for implementation during a crisis.
- Avoid evaluation instruments issued by special interest groups.
- Avoid evaluations by individuals not competent to make them.
- Avoid the mass distribution of findings; they may be distorted and used by the news media.
- Avoid accepting evaluation as a power play in collective bargaining.
- Avoid overstressing individual items apart from the context of the whole evaluation instrument.
- Avoid assigning the same value to different evaluations—examine the background of each respondent.
- Avoid making final recommendations based on evaluation material that only represents a part of the total picture.

There are a number of problems that need to be considered in evaluating two-year college administrators. One is the considerable amount of time that is required to develop, implement, and follow through on administrator evaluation. Objectivity on the part of the evaluator and the evaluated needs to be sought as much as possible. Being aware of the need for objectivity can assist in coming closer to achieving it.

The use of material in evaluations should be as open as confidentiality and common sense dictate. There are times when confidentiality serves the best interests of all parties. The results of appraisal interviews should be confidential, and this circumstance also should apply to any written correspondence.

Another problem can arise from tardy or non-communication of results of materials gathered as well as the interview itself. The credibility of the system can be significantly compromised by responses that are relatively superficial and late.

Summary

In the past, administrative evaluations completed on two-year college campuses have been more informal; however, today the concerned public as well as the faculty want to know that the people who "run things"

are evaluated also. Administrators should be accountable for their decisions that affect the college, especially when excellence/quality remains
a prominent agenda item on campuses.

There is not one major model or evaluation tool used in administrative evaluation, but we do know that the key to successful administrator
evaluation programs rests with the supervisor and subordinate. The
challenge in any form of evaluation is communication and planning.

Two-year colleges will continue to grow more complex administratively. Two-year colleges need to continue to define their missions, purposes, goals, and objectives. Perhaps two-year colleges are moving away
from being just about everything to everybody. A prominent agenda
item is excellence—in teaching, in faculties, in program offerings, and
in the operational aspects of the institution. Personal growth is also
pivotal to organizational improvement, as Wolotkiewics (1980, p. 39)
states: "The administrators should be assisted in their personal growth
which will be accompanied by an increase in the overall effectiveness of
the educational organization."

8

Evaluating External Relations

By Barbara Come and Charles E. Finley

Although higher education has generally acknowledged the value of positive external relations, it can also be said that most institutions have not developed a systematic approach to assessing how well they approach these tasks. Historically, many colleges and universities have merely assumed that the general public inherently understood and was supportive of higher education's mission. This comfortable state has been jolted as national concerns over increased tuition costs and skepticism about the quality of education are requiring college leaders to justify their institutions' operations (Palmer 1987). As a result, the ability of a college to be able to assess its various external relations activities has been elevated from desirable to crucial.

The task of establishing and maintaining positive external relations can be complicated for community colleges, for several of the reasons outlined by Young and Gwalamubisi (1986):

1. An institution's responsiveness to changing community needs can result in a school with a changing identity.
2. The current preoccupation with high status does not create a climate where two-year colleges serving those most in need in the community are highly valued.
3. Rarely are state and national decision makers graduates of community colleges, although this point is changing slowly.

4. Community colleges seldom sponsor events that draw regional or national media.
5. Many community colleges have allocated only modest resources to public relations and lobbying efforts.
6. By trying to be all things to all people, many community colleges have found that their comprehensive mission fragments their support.

In times of population growth, a community college could tolerate a blurred image; however, as Townsend (1986, p. 47) observes, "if students don't know how XXX Community College is different from YYY College or ZZZ Business Institute, then why should they choose it over the others?"

The impact of shrinking high school graduating classes may be further compounded by reduced willingness or ability on the part of federal, state, and local governments to amply fund public two-year schools. Bender and Daniel (1986) predict that this decrease in governmental allocations will force community colleges to seek greater support from an expanded range of constituent groups within their external environment.

State Governmental Relations

The need for community colleges to maintain positive governmental relations is inherent in their name, mission, and funding structure. Rowland (1986) contends that "responsibility for government relations must be at the highest levels of institutional administration." In the two-year college this statement means that government relations is the responsibility of the president or the primary responsibility of some other senior administrative officer. The responsibility for government relations must be clearly assigned and understood throughout the institution. Everyone needs to know who is responsible for contacting local congressional representatives, legislators, the mayor, and the governor. Since the state government is the primary source of funding for the two-year college, careful assessment of relationships with the governor's office and the state legislature is vital. Rowland (1986, p. 500) writes on three areas that need to be addressed when evaluating a school's governmental relations: Governmental action, or possible actions, that have, or can have, an impact, positive or negative, on the college and its ability to achieve its objectives. Second, the extent of the impact or how important a particular government action is to the institution. This assessment will help determine how much of an institution's resources ought to be committed to support its government relations effort in addition to the direction and timing of that effort. And, the necessary institutional resources needed to maximize the positive impact of a governmental action or minimize the negative; this requires strategy development and execution in the political arena.

To determine how well the government relations program at a two-year college is meeting the institution's objectives, Heemann (1985) for the Council for the Advancement and Support of Education (CASE) has developed a self-evaluation questionnaire that can be secured from this Washington-based organization.

Much recent legislation has been passed at the state level that pertains to forming partnerships between higher education, government, and business. Martorana and Garland (1984) point out that unemployment problems, which have plagued the states and the nation in the past, have begged for legislative attention. Because the two-year college mission is to provide vocational and technical training, it was a logical place for legislators to turn. The federally sponsored Job Training Partnership Act has provided monetary and administrative incentives for states to establish and revise training and retraining for dislocated workers, and occupational forecasting programs. And recent legislative attention to economic development has focused on the promotion of high-technology industries in the states.

To cite one successful example of two-year colleges, state government, and business partnerships: the Ohio Department of Development and the Ohio Board of Regents are working through the community colleges in collaboration with Ohio's businesses and industry with three goals: to establish Ohio as a world leader in innovation and entrepreneurial activity, to make Ohio's businesses more competitive in the world marketplace, and to leverage state and federal funds to accelerate new job creation in Ohio. This partnership has helped Ohio to move in four years from the position of 49th to 3rd in the nation in job creation; unemployment has been reduced from over 14 percent to 7.9 percent. Coulter also observes that the state's community colleges are "key players in this relationship because they provide the communication system and a strategically located delivery mechanism for technology transfer and training for Ohio's businesses, large and small."

In Maryland, state and local governmental agencies have developed a consortium and partnership with 15 community colleges. Although these colleges have been involved in training activities for their local regions, this coordinated effort enhances their collective potential to make a visible impact on statewide economic development. Representatives from the colleges, the Maryland Economic Development Office, and selected local economic development agencies work together to build an understanding of the community colleges' contributions and strengths in economic development. This model can be modified to fit the circumstances of any state seeking to develop a similar cooperative, coordinated effort.

Although the states currently are generating money for programs designed to help community colleges address economic development, competition for the funds is growing. Those institutions that find themselves recipients of these funds generally have a clear statement of direction for their economic development program, are creative, and have effective communications with the governor's office and key legislators. Constant evaluation of an institutions' relationship with the state government is vital if the institution wishes to compete successfully for monies being generated to encourage linkages between two-year colleges and business and industry. The following questions may be useful for this evaluative process:

- Has the college developed a clear, written statement of what it hopes to accomplish through its economic development plan? (Scott, p. 17).
- Has it been decided how best to use existing state resources? (ibid., p. 16).
- Have procedures been developed for determining priorities, especially when deciding between state and local needs?
- With the increasing volume of legislation regarding education/ business linkages, are there adequate sources of data and political intelligence to monitor issues of concern?
- Have clear-cut channels of authority and communications been developed for conducting government relations?
- Are key legislators invited to campus for activities such as tours, speaking engagements, and ceremonies? In this way, legislators can speak with students and learn firsthand about innovative programs on campus.
- Are the right people used to contact legislators at the right time?
- Are the active interests and involvement of advisory committees or legislative networks maintained?
- Are coalitions formed with other institutions and organizations to advance common interests on particular issues?

(Adopted from Jackson 1981; Rowland 1986; and Scott 1986-87.)

Local Governmental Relations

In many cases, operating and capital support for two-year colleges are partially dependent on a local tax base. Also, actions taken by a city council or a county board of supervisors can be extremely important to a community college. Public transportation, police and fire protection, local zoning ordinances, municipal utility systems, and exemptions from local property taxes are all local government issues that require the attention of two-year institutions. The manner in which an institution conducts itself as a member of the community can impact upon the way the institution is treated by the local government and the voters.

The following questions may be useful in assessing institutional relations with the local government: Does the institution maintain regular contact with local officials to discuss areas of mutual concern? If the institution is involved in an economic development program, does cooperation and support from the local government exist? Does respect and goodwill exist between the college and the local government? And, are periodic reports made to community leaders on the college's impact upon the local economy?

Business and Industry

Demographic and economic trends of the 1980s have brought about many societal changes which have greatly impacted American higher education, government, and business and industry. Two of these changes are especially noteworthy: (1) today there are fewer individuals in the 16 to 24 age bracket, and the military, higher education, and business are all competing for this sector of the population, and, (2) the competition in the international marketplace from high-technological countries with cheap labor has greatly increased (Garrison 1986-87, p. 20). The United States can only hope to compete by producing more for less while keeping quality high. In some cases, it is impossible to compete.

Two-year colleges and businesses have accepted the challenge to respond to these new realities; they have discovered that alliances can be beneficial to all parties. Colleges may increase enrollments, increase part-time staff, and enrich classroom instruction; and industry has found that two-year colleges can develop skilled workers at a lower cost than businesses through their own in-house training.

However, "just being involved" is not enough, and an ongoing institutional relationship with business and industry is desirable to answer key questions, such as, is the college determining training requirements to meet existing needs, and are relationships with existing employers effective enough to attract new jobs to the area? Only by a thorough assessment of present relationships with business and industry can two-year colleges expect to enhance their contacts with employers and to feel confident about the institution's standards of excellence and its responses to local employment needs.

A review of exemplary programs in several institutions may be useful toward a better understanding of the benefits of labor development programs. To develop an improved awareness of its business environment, Hagerstown Junior College (Maryland) places its faculty members in business and industrial work situations. This program has improved the school's understanding of the regional job economy and of the relationship between work force needs and regional labor conditions.

Many two-year colleges have launched assessment programs of employer needs such as Parkersburg Community College (West Virginia), Sinclair Community College (Ohio), and Atlantic Community College (New Jersey) where regional employers are asked to provide information about employee training needs, in-house educational programs, business recruitment practices, job trends, employee turnover rates, salary prospects by job category, and employment projections one to two years into the future. Employers also are asked to describe career interests and mobility patterns of employees, tuition incentive policies, knowledge about and use of college services, satisfaction with employed graduates of college programs, and willingness to assist the college in program planning (Fidler and others 1978).

Labette Community College (Kansas) is responding to local needs with project REFER (Relevant Education for Economic Recovery), which focuses on the current and future training needs of both the company and the individual employee. Courses are offered in the business and industrial sites as well as on campus. The comprehensive community college philosophy at Labette has produced escalating growth in enrollment, moving from 1,265 students in 1975 to 8,173 students in 1986.

The Oregon Small Business Development Center network and Lane Community College (Oregon) have responded to the needs of small businesses for management training by providing access to current information, training, resources, and management assistance services. Lane recognized the need for a strong small business community and established a business assistance center (BAC), which is a leading community resource. In 1983 the Oregon legislature recognized the success of Lane's effort to help small businesses and passed legislation that provided funding of $500,000 for the biennium and directed that a network of similar centers be developed to offer small business training and assistance at community colleges throughout the state.

By developing effective relationships with business and industry, two-year colleges can contribute to the economic development of their regions, states, and country, but also the colleges can benefit substantially from these linkages. When assessing labor development problems, individual institutions may find it useful to ask themselves questions such as: Has professional growth taken place on the part of administrators and faculty? Have initial training programs stimulated requests for further training? Is increased respect displayed by business and industry personnel toward community college faculty and staff? Has more efficiency and productivity in business translated into more tax support and greater enrollment for the college? (Fidler 1982).

Community Service

By definition, all community colleges are charged with providing service to their communities, but the diverse range of these services reflects profound differences in the communities and their perceived needs. College leaders and others who are interested in evaluating how well the college is meeting the needs of constituent groups can begin with some questions, such as:

1. To what extent has the college researched the community from a demographic standpoint? How is the population divided among age groups?
2. What minority groups comprise the service area and what are the projections for trends in ethnic composition?
3. What have been the social effects of changes in the area's economic base on various age groups and on minority groups?
4. With what area agencies might the college form linkages? Such a team approach could direct combined resources toward community needs.
5. Has the college created an image of being genuinely interested in understanding community needs? Do members of the community feel comfortable in coming to the college in search of solutions?
6. Are college facilities made available to the community wherever possible?
7. Does the college actively seek to produce programs and events that will be of interest to the community?

8. Have significant pockets of the college's constituency been ignored?
9. Do college-sponsored programs include offerings of interests to area minority groups?

One school that has made a strong effort to touch a broad spectrum of constituencies is Schoolcraft College in Michigan. College-sponsored workshops have brought thousands from the business sector onto the campus, and continuing education and community service programs have seen strong enrollment growth for their 200 yearly offerings. Schoolcraft also has designed an access-at-any-age policy that includes elementary school children in a talented-and-gifted program as well as senior citizens in fitness-after-fifty classes. Schoolcraft's community service mission extends beyond educational offerings. An annual speaker series along with musical, dramatic, and recreational programs, combined with the practice of making athletic fields available for a local soccer league reinforce Schoolcraft's image as a valued community resource (Schoolcraft 1986).

Cloud County Community College in Kansas conducted a survey of its service area and found that nearly one-quarter of its population was 65 years of age or older. The college responded to this community profile by developing an associate degree in gerontology (Hartman 1986).

Addressing a need within the urban constituency, Cuyahoga Community College (Ohio) offered a program to inner city high school students designed to improve their test-taking skills and enhance their chances for success at the postsecondary level (Palmer 1986). And in California, Bakersfield College established a women's reentry program with recruitment, orientation, advising, financial aid, child care, and job placement services (Osterkamp and Hullett 1983). These four schools exemplify the positive images that many community colleges have developed by first profiling their constituencies and then responding with appropriate resources.

Allocating Institutional Resources

Assessing the community service program can help presidents make prudent decisions on resource allocation. Many CEOs find themselves frustrated when dealing with the question of allocation in two ways: (1) the opportunities to become involved in external relations nearly always exceed the available resources, and (2) there are few quantifiable models for calculating which efforts will deliver the maximum yield. Nevertheless, colleges must still make hard decisions and periodically assess their wisdom.

One approach that is used is founded on the highly subjective sense that "this is the sort of things we ought to be doing." Often an analysis of a school's community service roles finds them traceable to the personal values of the president or trustees. When this is the case, periodic assessment plays a small role because the decision was not made on the basis of return-on-investment. Instead, a president might justify an institutional community service in terms of the number of people being served or the benefits derived by a given component of the community. In short, the yardstick becomes how much this investment will help the community.

At the other end of the spectrum is the CEO who sees the community service as another form of resource allocation and assumes a business-like approach. For this individual, the question is how much return the college will gain from its investment, viewing community service as an extension of the schools' marketing program and these efforts are assessed in terms of their potential for generating students. Having administrators join community service groups is viewed in terms of generating contacts with business leaders who may be in need of training services. Making college facilities available for public functions is seen as another vehicle for bringing people onto campus who might not otherwise have occasion to do so. One community college CEO phrased his approach to community service involvement in the form of a question: "I ask myself, 'How will doing this help my institution?'" With this approach, the yardstick is enrollment—either in credit courses or training developed for business and industry.

Major Participants in External Relations

Thus far this chapter has identified primary components of a community college's external environment: government, business and industry, and constituent groups within the service population. The next step involves an examination of key institutional personnel for interfacing with these groups. In short, is the institution overlooking any potential resources or avenues for improving external relations?

For most two-year colleges, five primary participants for external relations are the CEO, the board of trustees, foundation board, alumni, and the public relations office.

CEOs

Although everyone who works at the community college can do many things to promote the institution, the primary responsibility for enhancing the college's image belongs to the CEO. Because of this level of responsibility, his or her effectiveness in promoting quality external relations is imperative. The following questions may be helpful in assessing effectiveness: Is the CEO visible? Does he or she believe in and promote the organization, its products and services to those outside the institution? Does the CEO create an internal and external vision for the organization? To encourage relationships with business and industry, has the CEO identified local boards or committees that influence and direct the economic growth and development in the college's service area and sought status as a member of these boards? Does he or she give credit to others for their accomplishments? Does the CEO keep the lines of communication open between the college and external constituencies? Above all, is the CEO an expert communicator? Does he or she clearly convey the institution's mission, goals, and objectives to the many constituencies who influence and are influenced by the college?

Board of Trustees

Within the limitations of legislation, the trustees are responsible for operating the institution. As leaders in business, industry or the professions, trustees are viewed by the general public as individuals who have something to say about the institution. Because influential citizens are capable of having significant positive or negative impact upon the institution, the tact and integrity of trustees are sometimes tested. In order to assist in evaluating trustee performance in promoting quality external relations, the following questions may be asked:

1. With the understanding that public funding is not the only basis for supporting the institution, have trustees assisted the CEO in making long-range plans to enhance external relations that already exist at the institution?
2. Do the trustees play a team role in communicating with key legislators about institutional concerns?
3. Do the trustees belong to the Association of Community College Trustees and do they attend the annual convention of the association to help keep them abreast of current programs and models pertaining to colleges and their external constituents?
4. Do the trustees, working with the CEO, have a systematic and comprehensive method of monitoring legislation affecting the community college?
5. Do the trustees have appropriate liaison with department chairs

and program chairs to stay fully aware of new external relationships?

6. Are trustees careful not to promote programs in their own interests? Is the program for the good of the college?

Foundation Boards

Earlier in the chapter it was pointed out by Bender and Daniel (1986)
that the public favors increased giving by individuals and groups for
two-year colleges to supplement tax support. Recognizing this positive
public attitude, the number of foundations established by public two-
year colleges has tripled since 1974, but have the colleges viewed the
opportunities that are presented by foundations as another means for
improving community relations? By establishing foundation boards to
augment the official board of trustees, colleges can double the number
of influential community leaders closely involved with the institution.
Davis (1986) points out that foundation board members give credibility
to the institution and they can provide still another link between the
college and those whom the college can serve. By contacting business
and industrial leaders through a foundation office, the college has established still another channel for stating its case and enhancing its
image. The key to improved community relations through foundation
boards is careful selection of the board members and effective coordination of their efforts with the institution's comprehensive community
relations strategy.

Alumni Relations

Just as the creation of a foundation can provide a new channel for
enhancement of a community college's image, so can developing an
alumni association. A study by Sullenger (1976) found that nearly 90
percent of two-year college presidents placed a low priority on establishing an alumni relations program. The primary reason at that time for
rejecting an alumni program was the belief that it cannot generate
significant revenues. Although this logic remains largely valid, with
some exceptions such as Michigan's Delta College, an alumni association can more than pay its way as an avenue for enhancing public
relations. Kopecek and Kubrik (1982) report on research findings that
"more people learn more about community colleges from their family
and friends than in any other way." They further point out that through
an organization and/or publications, alumni can be "educated, encouraged, and mobilized to give information to others about the programs
and services of the college" (p. 77).

Several problems have traditionally plagued the efforts of two-year
schools to develop active alumni groups. First is the task of maintaining

current mailing lists. Many two-year colleges have experienced the dis-
appointment of seeing up to 80 percent of their mailings returned by
the post office. An institution needs to decide what level of success it is
willing to accept to justify the expense of developing, printing, and
mailing alumni communications. The degree to which alumni programs contribute to external relations usually depends on how imagi-
natively and extensively they are involved in the college's efforts.

Public Relations Office

Most community colleges have established a public relations office,
although they are distributed across a broad spectrum in terms of personnel qualifications, staffing, budget, and the scope of their missions.
This diversity may signal to some administrators that public relations
programs defy valid evaluation; however, some guidelines can be developed for this important function.

Slocum and Johnson (1977) assert that public relations (PR) efforts
need to begin with an analysis of the product and the setting of goals.
They point out that public relations goals must be both realistic and
quantifiable. Too often, however, the difficulty of quantifying goals results in PR efforts being measured by minutes of air time or column
inches of newspaper space. Because these are means to ends, more
valid goals might be a specific increase in a given program's enrollment
or a target number of inquiries being generated from a news release.

The same authors also offer four levels for evaluating a public relation's program. The first is based on intuitive judgment; the assumption
here is that no real method of assessment exists. The second is to
measure results in terms of visibility, such as using newspaper clippings
as a measure of success. The third involves multiple channels of communication being used with some measurable results, but precisely
which channels deserve the credit is not determined. The last level
occurs when a single channel generates a measurable result, but this is
seldom the case. When possible, a college should periodically change
only one factor in a campaign to allow this fourth level of evaluation.
Irrespective of the level of evaluation that a community college decides
is appropriate, the fundamental criterion against which a public relations office is measured is efficiency in resource allocation.

Summary

This chapter examines the increased need for positive external relations, the variety of constituent groups to be reached, the opportunities
and resources available to community colleges, and approaches to as-

sessing the effectiveness of the overall external relations effort. The common theme throughout the chapter is that external relations is too crucial to be assigned a low priority with respect to evaluation processes. In fact, the complexity of the external relations function points up the wisdom of establishing a formal evaluation procedure that allows persons with a broad base of expertise, both internal and external to the institution, to consider questions such as those posed within this chapter. Such an on-going assessment effort will allow the institution to maximize its potential for relating to its service area. The rewards for such an effort are both immediate and long term.

9

Evaluating Institutional Effectiveness

By Priscilla Haag-Mutter, Edward W. Holzapfel, Jr.
and C. Wayne Jones

B orn of democratic idealism, practicality, and demands of return-
ing World War II veterans attending college under the G.I. Bill
of Rights, the community college flourished through the 1950s,
60s, and 70s as increasingly diverse groups sought postsecondary education. In the rush to serve so many, two-year colleges had little time to
evaluate the effectiveness of their efforts. Most energy was put into
growth and diversification as clientele grew, changed, and demanded
more and varied educational programs.

For quite some time, the two-year college has been applauded for its
role in serving the postsecondary education needs of all Americans, but
more recently some leaders are questioning the wisdom of any institution trying to be everything to everyone. For example, Vaughn (1985,
p. 28) states, " . . . community colleges do not have the financial, physical, or intellectual resources to be all things to all people. Nor do they
have a public mandate to perform those functions for which they receive
no funding and that go well beyond their mission."

Purposes of Institutional Evaluation

To review, refine, and redefine the community college role, evaluation
became necessary. Cronbach (1980, p. 13) states that evaluation in general is undertaken for many reasons, including but not limited to: prior-

97

itizing possible courses of action, improving existing programs, maintaining quality, controlling subordinates, documenting financial necessity, eliciting support for a favorite project, and undercutting opponents' policies. No less can be said for the purpose and function of evaluation in higher education.

In 1980, the Carnegie Council on Policy Studies in Higher Education, concerned about the rapid changes that were affecting colleges and universities, suggested that the purpose of evaluation should be to contemplate and plan carefully for improvement of the quality of teaching, research, and service; preserve balance among the main academic efforts against counterforces of the educational marketplace; respond to academic consumer demands so that as little damage as possible is done to traditional academic programs; and develop creative means of offering new programs without accompanying increase in resources (Carnegie, p. 118).

The "Mortimer Report" (1984) said that the purposes of evaluation in higher education were to: "measure demonstrable improvements in student knowledge capacities, skills, and attitudes from entrance to graduation; insure that improvements occur within established, clearly expressed, and publicly announced and maintained standards of performance for awarding degrees; and demonstrate that improvements are cost-effective in use of student and institutional resources of time, effort and money" (p. 15).

Ewell (1987) summarizes the function and purpose of institutional evaluation programs as visible, integrated, on-going efforts governed by established policy, involving regular data collection and analysis. More than a network of resource and technical support for assessment, evaluation programs should serve as embodiments of an institution's commitment to self-examination and improvement. E. Boyer (1987, p. 262) wrote that only when we achieve greater clarity about a college's mission can we have standards that can be used as measures of our procedures. Only as college leaders clarify goals will they have the confidence to proceed with evaluation.

Problems with Institutional Evaluation

Assessing institutional effectiveness in the two-year college sector is difficult and ambiguous because of the ever-changing role of the institution. In its efforts to serve varied clientele (i.e., transfer students, single parents, re-entry adults, developmental students, corporate clients, retirees and senior citizens), the two-year college is sometimes criticized by those who say that access and quality are contradictory purposes; therefore, to evaluate their effectiveness community colleges need first to define (or to redefine) their missions, goals, and objectives. Cross (1985, p. 35) cites a survey (Duea 1981, p. 586) in which college presidents were asked to name the most critical issues facing their institutions at the time of the survey, and a decade into the future. Of the 20 issues listed, changing mission and purposes of their institutions was ranked fifth in current importance but second in importance among issues to be faced in 10 years.

Institutional Role Definition

To read many two-year institutions' mission statements is to suspect that they are indeed trying to be all things to all people and are diluting the quality of their programs and services. Two-year college leaders need to realistically appraise their institutions' place in the community. It may be necessary to cut some mediocre programs and trim, or combine, some outdated or redundant services in order to concentrate efforts and achieve higher overall quality.

Accreditation Domination

A second concern is that of letting accreditation evaluation take the place of all other assessment. The self-study and the preparation for accreditation visits are arduous and time-consuming, and faculty and staff often say they are over-burdened by the time and energy required for this effort. Administrators, staff, and faculty alike often object to additional self-initiated evaluation of any sort because of anxiety, overload, and resistance to change, yet other types of institutional evaluation are frequently more insightful and productive than external accreditation studies. Externally imposed evaluations are often thought to be toothless and/or self-serving, and often treated as ends rather than means to institutional improvement. Evaluation is most effective if it develops from internal concern for change and improvement.

High-Risk Students

In their study of Miami-Dade Community College, Roueche and Baker (1987), identified an issue at the core of problems encountered in assessing open admissions institutions—if community colleges should be judged the same as four-year colleges and faulted for their high attrition rates when many of their students are high-risk and may set unrealistic goals in relation to their skills and academic preparation. Clark (1980, p. 15) even suggests that a primary role of the community college is to provide a "cooling out" function for underprepared students. This period leads them to accept their academic limitations and decide to strive for more realistic academic and vocational goals. On the other hand, Parnell (1985, pp. 5-6) writes: "The comprehensive high school and the comprehensive community college work on the basis of a not-so-visible or dramatic definition of excellence. They seek the development of a highly diverse potential in all students."

Successful Evaluation Systems

The development of an institutional evaluation system, as proposed by Cronbach (1982, p. 7), is a continuing process. The essential ingredient is research and analysis conducted within a soundly constructed conceptual framework or model.

Institutional evaluation should be based on evidence and a standard of reference. Standards of reference that provide the greatest value in institutional evaluation come mainly from two sources: the individual institution, and collective institutions of a like nature, or benchmark institutions. For institutional standards, inquiry should be made in general areas such as objectives, goals, and mission statements; budgets; records of past performance; and policies, procedures, and directives. For collective standards, the evaluation should look to data supplied by benchmark institutions, accrediting associations, coordinating boards, federal agencies, and private groups. For one comprehensive approach to institutional evaluation, using "forty-five evaluative criteria," see Miller (1979, pp. 7-10). The following discussion includes the administration, planning, organization, information and communication, innovation, and staffing.

Administration

The administrative function at any institution is to provide direction and coordinate activities, and to set the guidelines within which progress can be made (Dressel 1976, p. 377). The quality of the administration is the prime determinant of an institution's effectiveness. An institutional evaluation, therefore, should include management policies, procedures, and operations. Despite their critical importance to institutional performance, administrators are secondary to the purposes for which the institution was organized. In the well-managed institution, administrative activity is more of an integrated whole that is "conspicuous" by its quiet and modest operating ways. But in poorly managed organizations, management is characterized more by the clamor and feverishness of crises and emergencies of which it is both the cause and the victim (Blanchard and others 1985, p. 43).

Planning

Every administrator has planning responsibilities and the effectiveness of the institution will be affected to the degree that skills in constructing sound and realistic plans are developed. The following questions can assist in evaluating an institution's planning process: Is the plan far-reaching; are the plans institution-centered; does the plan have positive goals; is the plan based on careful appraisal; does the plan require specific results; does the plan have a realistic timetable; does the plan identify the person/group responsible; and does the plan lay the basis for evaluation?

Organization

An effective organizational structure has procedures for testing each function and activity for its relevance to the mission and objectives. Indicators of organizational effectiveness would include: an adequate enrollment to support the organization; sound fiscal health and freedom from serious illnesses; a positive public image; an attraction for, and the ability to hold, a strong management team; prudent use of human and material resources; effective coordination of various programs and activities with a minimum of duplication, with strong mutual support, and a minimum of non-productive internal conflict; application of the institution's management talent to high-priority opportunities and problems; and assists administrators in applying their highest skills to the opportunities in their areas of responsibility for the largest portion of their time.

To appraise organizational effectiveness, it may be instructive to consider indicators of a potentially deficient organization, which include: frequent changes in the organizational plan, lack of arrangement for administrative succession, late decisions, inadequate information, impossibility of accountability, excessive tenure, excessive communicating, tolerance of incompetence, and obvious wage and salary inequities.

Information and Communication

The success of an educational institution is greatly affected by the quality of information available to it, and the efficiency of its internal and external communications. Only some confidential and sensitive information should be closely held; therefore, if an institutional evaluation tends to treat a great many things as confidential a major problem possibly has been uncovered.

Innovation

Innovative institutions are characterized by freely moving knowledge of what is happening in and out of the institution (Peters and Waterman 1982, p. 193). Non-innovative institutions, on the other hand, show sharp breaks in the flow of knowledge and information between the top, middle, and lower levels of management. Successful innovation may involve subsequent changes in procedures, policies, systems management philosophy, and organizational relationships.

Staffing

The mission of an institution's staffing function is to maximize the return on its investment in personnel, and effectiveness can be judged by the degree that its employees act in support of the institution's objectives. Open communication can positively impact upon work performance by having available items such as mission statement, management philosophy, goals and objectives, detailed plans, policies, procedures, rules and regulations, bulletins, and job descriptions.

The final evaluation of an institution's effectiveness is based upon the results achieved. The following model is suggested as a means for assessing the achievement of institutional effectiveness.

An Institutional Evaluation Model

This comprehensive model for two-year colleges considers major phases of institutional functioning, with special emphasis on outcome measures. It is a dynamic model that provides feedback for constant adjustment of both educational and assessment processes.

The model (Figure 5) is divided into three distinct phases which provide for a continuous flow of assessment processes and information, and which also can be integrated with an institutional planning process. This latter factor is important because the assessment process should become an integral part of the institutional functioning without creating an additional assessment superstructure and thus adding to costs.

The Pre-Assessment Phase

For the institution just beginning the development of an assessment process, this is the most important phase. Without proper planning and implementation at this point, the remainder of the processes is failure-prone no matter how rational or well-designed it may be. This phase

AN INSTITUTIONAL EVALUATION SYSTEM
FOR TWO-YEAR COLLEGES

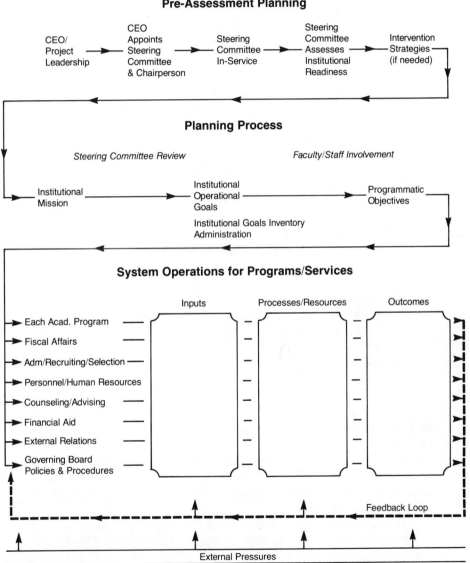

Figure 5

sets the stage both in terms of project leadership and motivation of the institution's faculty and staff.

The CEO and the leadership role. The observable behavior of the CEO will do much more to motivate the staff and to win acceptance of the project than will mere verbalization of procedures and platitudes concerning the importance of assessment (Reitz 1987, p. 311). Because of the significant impact of the project on the entire campus, the CEO needs to be seen as providing active leadership throughout the process. Operational tasks can be delegated but leadership responsibility cannot. According to Ewell (1984, p. 8), it is not enough to know the probable linkages between learning factors and learning outcomes; it is necessary to know how to induce institutions to build the requisite kinds of commitments and to make the kinds of structural changes necessary. These tasks are clearly a major role for the CEO.

The steering committee: Appointments. A steering Committee needs to be appointed which is representative of the internal constituencies who will be involved in the assessment project and who will be affected by its outcomes. The composition of this committee will be determined by the specific campus structure; however, some generalized statements about representation can be made. Because the curriculum will become the focal point of the assessment (ibid., p. 72), the chief academic officer and appropriate faculty representation should be present. Other senior level administrators responsible for support and student services also should be appointed. The Steering Committee needs to be large enough to represent key constituencies but not so large as to become unwieldy. The committee's responsibility is to provide direction and control for the process, not to perform the complete evaluation. The CEO probably should appoint himself or herself to the Steering Committee in keeping with the leadership role, although the institution's size and nature need to be considered.

Steering committee: In-service. Providing training in the techniques and concepts of evaluation for those people charged with directing the process is a next step, and extra resources will be needed. The desire and commitment to carry out the project should not be confused with having the ability to do so. The committee needs to become familiar with the processes of the assessment model and the technology of the measurement systems.

Assessing institutional readiness. Kells (1983, p. 37) suggests several design questions in dealing with institutional evaluation. These questions can facilitate assessing the readiness of the institution to undertake self-assessment. The status of the following factors should be studied by the Steering Committee at the outset of the assessment process: institutional research capabilities, master planning activities, clear statement of goals, availability of recent and useful self-study processes, rate of personnel turnover, morale and campus political factors, consensus among formal and informal campus leaders concerning the major problems facing the institution, psychological readiness of the staff, other accreditation relationships, and accommodations needed relative to the size and complexity of the institution.

Intervention strategies. Based on the findings of the Readiness Assessment, some strategies may be necessary to correct the identified institutional deficiencies. Proceeding without this step, or ignoring the results of it, can cause failure for the rest of the project. This juncture represents a key reason why the CEO should be involved in supporting the process. It will be his or her ultimate responsibility to judge what measures to take in moving the institution toward readiness, including delaying the implementation of the next phase.

The Planning Phase

When the Pre-Assessment Phase has been completed and the decision has been made to move forward, the Planning Phase is implemented under the direction of the Steering Committee. Attention to the Planning Phase is critical because the model places special emphasis on outcomes. Without careful planning, clear statements of intent cannot be developed, and valid measurements of outcomes are not possible without definition of outcomes.

Steering Committee Reviews: Institutional Mission. The Steering Committee reviews the institutional mission statement, and makes any desirable adjustments; specifically, the committee should evaluate the extent to which these three factors are present and well-defined (Carruthers and Lott 1981, p. 26):

1. *Statement of mission.* A broad statement of the fundamental purpose of the institution, often containing some value statement concerning the outcomes the institution wishes to produce;
2. *Role definition.* A statement which differentiates the institution from other types of institutions; and
3. *Scope.* Specifies the range of activities to be undertaken by the institution.

Because the mission statement provides a public pronouncement about the reasons for the institution's existence, the Steering Committee should seek institution-wide input during its review or development. CEO leadership is needed at this stage to underscore the importance of quality involvement.

Institutional operational goals. The goals are necessary to operationalize the mission statement. They provide a set of circumstances sought in pursuit of the mission (ibid., p. 28), and they provide the broad framework for developing the specific objectives to be accomplished by the institution in fulfilling its mission.

Faculty and staff involvement. While selected faculty and staff have been involved to this point in the mission review and development process, more general involvement of faculty and staff becomes paramount to accomplish the final step in the planning phase. At the unit level the objectives that will fulfill the operational goals, and ultimately the mission, need to be developed. The unit level provides the building blocks for institutional functioning. The assessment of institutional effectiveness is the measure of how the units combine to produce the desired outcomes.

Units of analysis. Before a rational set of objectives can be developed, the units should be identified which will accurately define the function of the institution. These units will be defined according to the mission and structure of the institution; however, some standard units should be examined, such as each academic department, academic support services, the various student services functions, fiscal affairs, and facilities.

Programmatic objectives. The development of objectives for each unit is key to the assessment process, stating the desired outcomes which the unit should address in furthering the education of the students. The setting of internal standards is the first step toward external accountability (Ewell 1984, p. 4). These intended outcomes will be measured against actual outcomes and, therefore, should be developed through careful deliberations by the personnel in the unit. If the staff has not previously developed programmatic objectives, an in-service program may be desirable. The objectives need to be constructed so that they lead to outcomes which can be measured.

Program and Services Operations Phase

This third phase of the model assesses unit functions. When the objectives have been determined, the inputs, processes, and outcomes can be assessed. While the assessment of outcomes is the primary function of the model, the input and process factors cannot be ignored because they provide the resources that result in outcomes.

Inputs. The assessment of the inputs examines those factors which are necessary for the unit to produce the desired outcomes. Examples of criteria for a technology program would be the adequacy of the unit budget, the appropriateness of faculty credentials and qualifications, the adequacy of instructional equipment and materials, and the quality of advisory committee input. The full range of criteria is developed based on the functions of the specific unit being assessed.

Processes. The processes are the dynamics which occur as the unit performs its various activities. Examples of processes to be examined for the technology program would be an analysis of the teaching and learning styles found in the department, the extent and uses of instructional support services, student evaluation measures, and faculty professional development activities.

Outcomes. Objectives, inputs, and processes are essential in their own rights, but their importance in this model lies in their abilities to support outcomes. Institutions do not exist for the purpose of collecting inputs or developing processes, they exist to produce outcomes which are positive changes in the cognitive and affective performance of students. Consequently, the "bottom line" of this model is an evaluation of the outcomes produced. Accountability, quality, and excellence are concepts that speak to the results produced by the educational process.

Assessments relying on outcome measures can be placed into two general categories—those that measure achievement against an absolute standard and those that measure achievement as relative gain (Ewell 1984, p. 18). The former is an assessment of standards comparison, while the latter is an assessment of change and requires a baseline measurement. A professional certifying exam is an example of comparison against a standard; the value-added approach is an example of assessing change.

These two approaches lead to the need to recognize the valuation process at work in assessment. When assessing outcomes against an external standard, a value is being placed on the outcome and that the standard presumably is valued by the faculty or staff; therefore, care needs to be taken to examine the values at work when selecting standards against which to assess outcomes. Are the standards valid measures of outcomes based on the mission and goals of the institutions, and on the programmatic objectives?

Some pitfalls also can exist in the measurement of change. There is usually only one right answer, that being the measure of change (ibid.). If a student gains 20 points on a standardized mathematics test, a quality enhancement has taken place, provided that the test has some validated relevancy to the curriculum.

An assessment of outcomes should provide for both kinds of measurements in order to provide a comprehensive picture of the effectiveness of the system. The measurement of change through a value-added process provides a good quality control mechanism, while comparison against an absolute standard allows the value systems of internal and external constituencies to interact in the process. The scope of this paper does not allow for the detailed listing of outcomes measures; however, the outcomes should follow logically from whatever objectives are set for the unit.

The Feedback Loop

The feedback loop is the mechanism that provides for the dynamic functioning of this assessment model, and also is the part which integrates the model into the routine functioning of the institution. Once the outcome measurements have been taken and compared with the unit programmatic objectives, the results are given to the unit. Based on the results, objectives can be clarified or adjusted at the Planning Phase to influence the functioning of the program and services operations. The feedback cycles through the Operations Phase to allow adjustment to the input and process factors. After an appropriate time lapse, the outcomes are again assessed and the information is worked through the system once more.

This model is information based, meaning that knowledge of results is necessary in order to have meaningful impact on the institution. The development of the institutional research capability is necessary; however, much of the information needed may already exist in different parts of the institution, or in the computerized management information system. The task is to integrate these data in one place, and then use them in a systematic way to improve the functioning of the institution. In the end, institutional improvement should be the goal in using this, or any other, model of assessment.

Summary

The development of an institutional evaluation system is a continuing process. Central to this concept is the belief that administrators need an early warning system for the detection of potentially destructive problems, and for the identification of opportunities for improvement. The problems facing two-year institutions and their administrators are so variegated and sophisticated that every institution should provide its administrators with recent and valid information about current circumstances. A systematic and integrated institutional evaluation process can be an efficient and effective source for such information.

Institutions that have not yet developed some objective bases for measuring their performance could be on their way to future troubles. For example, since most two-year colleges are enrollment driven, it is important to have sufficient and reliable indicators for predicting enrollments. Without these data, administrators may spend more time on looking good than being good, and unless a technique such as institutional evaluation is applied, the difference may not be detected until irreparable damage has been done.

Caution, however, should be exercised in making comparisons with other institutions. The myth of the "typical" institution is dispelled in the findings of Dickmeyer (1987) who found that no group of institutions exist whose data show them to be completely "typical." Institutions should, therefore, strive to discover what makes them unique and not to be pressured toward some nonexistent "median" performance. Dickmeyer concluded, "Diversity is clearly a characteristic—and no doubt a great strength—of community and junior colleges" (p. 4). Uniqueness, however, needs to be tempered as Cartter (in Millett 1980, pp. 4-5) cautions, "diversity can be a costly luxury if it is accompanied by ignorance." Therefore, an information-based assessment system is a meaningful way to evaluate the effectiveness of institutional outcomes.

10

The Future Role of Evaluation

By Charles E. Finley

C ommunity college leaders who are concerned about the future role of the evaluation function for their institutions will want to address the recent themes and current issues in higher education. From this perspective, some future trends and directions can be extrapolated.

Just as the themes of the 1960s were freedom and participation, and the 1970s were marked by moves toward greater accountability, Deegan (1988) views the 1980s as the decade of concern for quality and productivity, with a renewed emphasis on educational standards. It is his sense that these themes will carry over well into the 1990s and, if so, one can expect the evaluative function to continue to grow in importance among institutional priorities. To gain a sharper focus on the evaluation process, one can study predictions of the issues that will be facing community colleges at the end of this century.

Economic and Demographic Issues

Deegan sees economic and demographic issues influencing higher education. He notes that:

1. By 1990, America will have six million fewer teenagers than only 10 years earlier.
2. Between 1985 and 1995, there will be an 18 percent drop in traditional college age Americans.
3. These patterns will produce keen competition between the business community and military for young people.

Two predictable impacts of these issues on the evaluation function of community colleges are increased concern about the effectiveness of external relations (specifically, marketing), and about program assessment. Relative to the latter impact, retention strategies may become more important as projected enrollment competition influences colleges to emphasize quantitative models.

A second age group to be watched is the 35-44 age range, which from 1980 to 1990 is projected to increase by 42 percent; however, the number of middle management positions are estimated to increase by only 19 percent. The increasing competition by the 10.4 million people in this age group for management positions may cause many individuals to find their upward mobility blocked and to seek alternative careers.

The need for job retraining will increase as America's share of world manufacturing continues to decline. Between 1979 and 1984, 11 million Americans lost their jobs and, of these workers, 20 percent are estimated to require improved basic skills before they can expect jobs with advancement potential. The national shift away from manufacturing will create jobs in other sectors. Vaughn (1983) writes that people today must find employment in new and technically demanding fields which were not available in high schools.

An American Association of Community and Junior Colleges' teleconference (The American Seminar, 1987) reported still more data that further underscores a growing need for retraining in the future:

- The average worker will change jobs nearly seven times and change occupations three times.
- From 1985 to the year 2000, the proportion of 16 to 24 year olds will shrink from 30 percent of the population to 16 percent.
- Seventy-five percent of those who will be working in the year 2000 are already in the workplace.
- America's budget for training and development is currently at $210 billion; however, small businesses, unlike major corporations, cannot afford to do their own training.
- Millions of America's workers lack the basic skills needed for future retraining.

Increasing Need for Retraining

A major force in the need for retraining is the knowledge explosion. As of 1987, 90 percent of the world's scientific knowledge was unknown only 30 years previously and this present body of knowledge is expected to double by the year 2000 (AACJC 1987). The pace of knowledge production will quicken; Brazziel (1981) estimated that the volume of scientific and technical information will double every eight years.

These trends point to a profound and ongoing need for retraining; the need for training and development has already created a major industry. Moon (1981) observes that only about 12 million American adults are educated in colleges and universities while more than three times as many are trained elsewhere. In fact, AACJC cites figures that show the total annual budget for training and development in America is $210 billion, an amount rapidly nearing the $238 billion budget for formal education. A major share of this training and development budget is provided by America's 300 largest corporations, even though 90 percent of the new jobs created in the last decade were with businesses too small to perform their own training.

Community colleges will be able to meet the training needs of American business if several components of their operations can be effectively assessed, such as:

1. Institutional effectiveness to assure that the expansion of one college function does not impair its more traditional missions.
2. Relations with business and industry to provide clear communication lines.
3. Academic programs to measure flexibility and relevance.
4. Part-time faculty to respond to the often increased role of this group in providing short-term training.
5. Student services to meet the special needs of non-traditional full-time students seeking retraining. Ironically, the dramatic growth of this component of the community college mission may occur at a time when two crucial resources are lacking—faculty and laboratory equipment.

The Graying of College Faculty

The "graying" of college faculty is likely to become a major concern in the 1990s. A 1983 California study (Deegan 1988) revealed 40 percent of that state's full-time faculty were at least 50 years of age, and over 20 percent were over 55; the current surplus of college teachers in certain parts of the nation can be expected to disappear soon. With fewer people available to hire, staff development will become even more important. Two books, although written for four-year institutions, offer some excellent research and insights into these matters: Bowen and Schuster, *American Professors*, 1986; and Eble and McKeachie, *Improving Undergraduate Education Through Faculty Development*, 1985.

The second crucial resource at risk is laboratory equipment. Another California survey (Chancellor's Office 1985) found 67 percent of equipment used in occupational programs was either somewhat or seriously out of date. Only comprehensive approaches to program evaluation will reveal these inadequacies in time to correct them through systematic planning and budgeting.

Clearly, attracting new faculty and replacing equipment will place demands on financial resources. Deegan predicts, however, that four factors—the federal budget deficit, new competition for dollars, changing public attitudes, and an aging population—will combine to reduce taxpayer support in the 1990s to a level of inadequacy. The resulting financial squeeze would require postsecondary institutions to assess their abilities to discover new ways to generate resources, link with agencies and other schools, and share expensive technologies. All three ventures will serve as tests of the institution's ability to utilize strong external relations in adapting to scarce funds. Vaughn (1983) sums up the dynamic: "Flexibility will have to be accomplished by change rather than growth" (p. 247).

Greater Accountability

Another issue of continuing concern is accountability. The movement toward merit pay will not dissipate in the near future unless a significant recession occurs nor will the importance of a valid faculty evaluation system. Concern for accountability will continue to bring student evaluation processes under scrutiny as well. For community colleges, the double challenge will be to raise standards while maintaining access.

If politicians continue to respond to public concerns over standards in higher education, the 1990s may see a continued growth in statewide testing. An example that is already in operation is Florida's College Level Academic Skills Test (CLAST) which must be passed after completion of the freshman and sophomore years before students in public colleges can earn an associate of arts degree or be granted junior-year status (Evangelauf 1985). College leaders who view these legislated standards as a response to perceived complacency on the part of individual programs or postsecondary institutions, may be motivated to strengthen both their program and student evaluation programs before their state governments decide to impose stricter mandates.

The trend for accountability is accompanied by a mandate for community colleges to maintain or even improve access to higher education for economically and socially disdvantaged persons. According to Hodgkinson (1985) there will be room for improvement in the 1990s. He observes that from 1975 to 1982 there was a 29 percent increase in the graduation of black students from high school; however, black college enrollment actually dropped by 14 percent for the same seven years. The same discrepancy occurred among Hispanic Americans with a 38 percent increase in high school graduation, but a college enrollment decrease of 16 percent.

Serving Economically Deprived Students

Historically, economically disadvantaged and minority students have looked to community colleges for educational opportunity. By 1978, two-year colleges were enrolling 42 percent of America's black students and more than half of Hispanic and American Indian students (U.S. National Center for Educational Statistics 1982). However, this upward trend began to reverse itself the following year as community college enrollments shifted to reflect the population at large. Hodgkinson attributes part of this trend to increasing numbers of talented minority youth taking advantage of the military's educational programs, but this is only one factor. Templin (1983) warns of the threat posed by this trend: "Should the transition of the community college to a middle class college occur, will it be at the expense of the lower-income and disadvantaged student?" (p. 48).

Answers to this question will be founded on resource allocation decisions which, in turn, will reflect the institution's mission. Being caught between mandates both for higher quality and for increased access will require community colleges to assess their missions and their institution's adherence to those missions.

Educating the Whole Person

Still another test of institutional evaluation will come from a growing concern over what students are required to learn. E. Boyer (1986) raises three questions that he sees impacting on future community college agendas. First, what will it mean "to be an educated person in the year

2000 and beyond?" (p. 15). Second, how can colleges ensure that students acquire "not just knowledge through technology but the wisdom to interpret the knowledge?" (p. 16). Third, how can community colleges help students "see more clearly the connections between what they learn and how they live?"

Relative to this last issue, Boyer sees a current body of students characterized by self-centeredness and inadequate ties to the community at-large. He cites two studies of Carnegie college students in which 64 percent indicate career success as their most important goal; only 48 percent list spiritual fulfillment as a key objective in their lives; and 70 percent said being financially wealthy was very important, but only 45 percent said developing a meaningful philosophy of life was an important goal. Boyer concludes that our colleges are "bankrupt if our students understand their own individual talents and see no connections to their fellow human beings, both in this nation and around the world." The issue of defining the word "educated," will generate debate and serve as a catalyst for program, student, and even institutional evaluation.

Boyer's observation places in perspective the crucial balance that exists between a community college's evaluation function and its charge to remain responsive. Since its conception, the community college has consistently changed to accommodate rapid shifts in America's economy, demographics, and lifestyles. Such a kinetic existence can lure an institution into the maze of nebulous functions and a blurred mission. Future social and economic forces can be counted on to impact the community college's identity well into the next century. However, those schools with viable evaluation programs already in place will have the ability to view themselves from a clear perspective, continually assess their progress, and make course corrections along the way.

Bibliography

ACCTion Consortium. 1982. *Master teacher assessment and professional growth*. Pendleton, SC: Tri-County Technical College.

ACCTion Consortium. 1983. *Tri-county technical college: Teaching faculty perception inventories*. Pendleton, SC: Tri-County Technical College.

ALEXANDER, J. M., AND J. S. STARK. 1986. Focusing on student academic outcomes (A working paper). Ann Arbor: National Center for Research to Improve Postsecondary Teaching and Learning.

American Association of State Colleges and Universities. 1976. Resource center for planned change. *Program Evaluation*. Washington, DC: AASCU.

American Association of State Colleges and Universities. 1984. *In pursuit of degrees with integrity*. Washington, DC: AASCU.

The American seminar: Teleconference program. 1987. Washington, DC: AACJC.

ANDREWS, H. A. 1985. *Evaluating for excellence*. Stillwater, OK: New Forums Press.

ANDREWS, H. A., AND W. A. MARZANE. 1983-1984, December/January. Faculty evaluation: Stimulates expectations of excellence. *Community and Junior College Journal*. 35-57.

ARMOUR, R. 1979, October 15. What do they expect of me? *The Chronicle of Higher Education*. 48.

117

ARNS, R. G., AND W. POLAND. 1980. Changing the university through program review. *Journal of Higher Education*. 51: 268-284.

ARREOLA, R. 1983. Establishing successful faculty evaluation and development programs. *In*: Evaluating faculty and staff. New directions for community colleges, ed. A. Smith. 41: 83-94. San Francisco: Jossey-Bass.

ASTIN, A. W. 1982. Why not try some new ways of measuring quality? *Educational Record*. 63: 10-15.

ASTIN, A. W. 1983. Strengthening transfer programs. *In*: Issues for community college leaders in a new era. G. B. Vaughan and Associates. San Francisco: Jossey-Bass.

BANTA, T. W., AND H. S. FISHER. 1987, March 4. Measuring how much students have learned entails much more than simply testing them. *The Chronicle of Higher Education*. 44-45.

BARAK, R. J. 1982. *Program review in higher education*. Boulder, CO: National Center for Higher Education Management.

BARAK, R. J. 1986. Common myths in program review. *Educational Record*. 67: 52-54.

BARATTA, M. K. 1976, July. A program review model to determine which programs require in-depth evaluation. Paper presented to the annual meeting of the North Central Region AERA/SIG Community/Junior College Research, Madison, WI.

BEHRENDT, R. L., AND M. H. PARSONS. 1983. Evaluation of part-time faculty. *In*: Evaluating faculty and staff. New directions for higher education, ed. A. Smith. 41. San Francisco: Jossey-Bass.

BENDER, L., AND D. DANIEL. 1986. Rethinking funding strategies: Integrated planning and resource development for the small two-year college of 1990. *Community, Junior, and Technical College Journal*, 57: 22-25.

BERGQUIST, W. H., AND G. J. TENBRINK. 1978. Evaluation of administrators. *International encyclopedia of higher education*. 4: 1493-1498. San Francisco: Jossey-Bass.

BILES G. E., AND H. P. TUCKMAN. 1986. *Part-time faculty personnel management policies*. New York: Macmillan.

BISESI, M. 1984. Program evaluation: A qualitative planning tool. *Planning and Changing*. 15: 144-151.

BLACKBURN, R. T., AND M. J. CLARK. 1975. An assessment of faculty performance: Some correlates between administrator, colleague, student, and self-ratings. *Sociology of Education*. 48: 242-256.

BLANCHARD, K., ZIGARMI, P., AND ZIGARMI, D. 1985. *Leadership and the one minute manager*. New York: William Morrow & Co.

BLEE, M. R. 1985, October/November. Is statewide exit testing for community college students a sound idea? Point. *AACJC Journal*. 52-53.

BLOOM, A. 1987. *The closing of the American mind*. New York: Simon and Schuster.

BNA Editorial Staff. 1972. *Grievance Guide*. Washington, DC: The Bureau of National Affairs, Inc.

BOGGS, G. R. 1984. A response to uncertainty: The increased utilization of part-time instructors in American community colleges. *Community/Junior College Quarterly*. 8: 5-17.

BOWEN, H. R. 1974. Accountability: Some concluding comments. *In*: Evaluating institutions for accountability. New directions for institutional research, ed. H. R. Bowen. San Francisco: Jossey-Bass.

BOWEN, H. R., AND J. H. SCHUSTER. 1986. *American professors: A national resource imperiled*. New York: Oxford University Press.

BOYER, C. M., AND A. C. MC GUINNESS. 1986. Recent state initiatives to improve the quality of undergraduate education. *State Education Leader*. 5: 12.

BOYER, E. 1986. Toward the year 2000 and beyond: A community college agenda. *Community, Junior, and Technical College Journal*. 57: 14-17.

BOYER, E. 1987. *College: The undergraduate experience in America*. New York: Harper and Row.

BOYER, M. 1973. Teacher evaluation: Toward improving instruction. *In*: Toward instructional accountability: A practical guide to educational change, eds. J. Roueche and B. Herrscher. 186-191. Palo Alto, CA: R. R. Donnelley & Sons.

BRAMLETT, P., AND R. C. RODRIQUEZ. 1982-1983. Part-time faculty: Full-time concern. *Community and Junior College Journal*. 53: 40-41.

BRASKAMP, L. A. 1982. Evaluation systems are more information systems. *In*: Designing academic program reviews. New directions for higher education, ed. R. F. Wilson. San Francisco: Jossey-Bass.

BRASKAMP, L. A., BRANDENBURG, D. C., AND ORY, J. C. 1984. *Evaluating teaching effectiveness: A practical guide*. Beverly Hills: Sage Publications.

BRAZZIEL, W. F. 1981. College-corporate partnerships in higher education. *Educational Record*. 62: 50-53.

BROWN, R. D. 1978. Implications of new strategies for accountability in student affairs. *Journal of College Student Personnel*. 9: 123-126.

BURCK, H. D., AND G. W. PETERSON. 1975. Needed: More evaluation, not research. *Personnel and Guidance Journal*. 53: 563-569.

CAHN, S. M. 1987, October 14. Faculty members should be evaluated by their peers, not by their students. *The Chronicle of Higher Education*. B2-B3.

Carnegie Council on Policy Studies in Higher Education. 1980. *Three thousand futures: The next twenty years in higher education*. San Francisco: Jossey-Bass.

CARRUTHERS, J., AND G. LOTT. 1981. *Mission review: Foundation for strategic planning*. Boulder, CO: National Center for Higher Education Management Systems.

CASHIN, W. E. 1983. Concerns about using student ratings in community colleges. *In*: Evaluating faculty and staff. New directions for higher education, ed. A. Smith 57-66. San Francisco: Jossey-Bass.

CASTETTER, W. B., AND R. S. HEIGHER. 1971. Appraising and improving the performance of school administrative personnel. *Administrative Evaluation*. Richmond, VA: Higher Education Leadership and Management Society. 47-50.

CATANZARO, J. 1987, February/March. Counterpoint. *AACJC Journal*. 53.

CENTRA, J. A. 1972. The utility of student ratings for instructional improvement. Project Report 72-16. Princeton, NJ: Educational Testing Service.

CENTRA, J. A. 1975. Colleagues as raters of classroom instruction. *Journal of Higher Education*. 46: 327-337.

CENTRA, J. A., ed. 1977. The how and why of evaluating teaching. *In*: Renewing and evaluating teaching. New directions for higher education. 93-107. San Francisco: Jossey-Bass.

CENTRA, J. A. 1979. *Determining faculty effectiveness*. San Francisco: Jossey-Bass.

Chancellor's Office. 1985. Board of Governors. California Community Colleges. *Contours of change*. Sacramento, CA.

Change in America. 1986, September 17. *The Chronicle of Higher Education*. 1.

CHURCHMAN, D. 1980. The role of evaluation in the two-year college. *Community/Junior College Research Quarterly*. 4: 241-247.

CLARK, B. R. 1980. The "cooling out" function revisited. *In*: Questioning the community college role. New directions for community colleges, ed. G. B. Vaughn. 32. San Francisco: Jossey-Bass.

CLOWES, D. A. 1981. Community college program review: A model. *Community College Review*. 9: 3-9.

COHEN, A. M., PALMER, J. C., AND ZWEMER, K. D. (1986). *Key resources on community colleges*. San Francisco: Jossey-Bass.

COHEN, P. A., AND W. J. MC KEACHIE. 1980. The role of colleagues in the evaluation of college teaching. *Improving College and University Teaching*. 28: 147-154.

Colleges prodded to prove worth. 1987, January 18. *New York Times*. 1.

COULTER, W. 1987, January 15. In a letter to the American Association for Community and Junior Colleges (AACJC) presidents.

CRABBS, M. A., AND S. C. CRABBS. 1978. Counseling center evaluation:

Alternative strategies. *National Association of Student Personnel Administrators Journal*. 6: 41-47.

CRONBACH, L. J. 1982. *Designing evaluations of educational and social programs*. San Francisco: Jossey-Bass.

CRONBACH, L. J., AND ASSOCIATES. 1980. *Toward reform of program evaluation: Aims, methods, and institutional arrangements*. San Francisco: Jossey-Bass.

CROSS, K. P. 1985. Determining missions and priorities for the fifth generation. *In*: Renewing the American community college, eds. W. L. Deegan and D. Tillery. San Francisco: Jossey-Bass.

CUTLER, E. 1984, November. Open for business. *AACJC Journal*. 28-30.

DAVIS, B. 1986. What community colleges do to increase private giving. *Community, Junior, and Technical College Journal*. 57: 35-36.

DEEGAN, W. L. 1988, in press. *External forces that will influence education in the decade ahead*. New Directions for Community Colleges. San Francisco: Jossey-Bass.

DICKMEYER, N. 1987. *Comparative financial statistics for public community and junior colleges*. Washington, DC: NACUBO.

DRESSEL, P. L. 1976. *Handbook of academic evaluation*. San Francisco: Jossey-Bass.

DUEA, J. 1981. President's views on current and future issues in higher education. *Phi Delta Kappan*. 62: 586-588.

DZIECH, B. W., ed. 1986. *Controversies and decision making in different economic times*. San Francisco: Jossey-Bass.

EBLE, K. E., AND W. J. MC KEACHIE. 1985. *Improving undergraduate education through faculty development*. San Francisco: Jossey-Bass.

ERTEL, H. C. 1980. Advisory committees for development and program review in teacher education. *Journal of Business Education*. 55: 166-167.

EVANGELAUF, J. 1985, July 3. Sophomores in Florida public colleges must pass a new test of their academic skills. *The Chronicle of Higher Education*.

EWELL, P. T. 1983. *Information on student outcomes: How to get it and how to use it*. Boulder, CO: National Center for Higher Education Management Systems.

EWELL, P. T. 1984. *The self-regarding institution: Information for excellence*. Boulder, CO: National Center for Higher Education Management Systems.

EWELL, P. T. 1985a. Some implications for practice. *In*: Assessing educational outcomes, ed. P.T. Ewell. San Francisco: Jossey-Bass.

EWELL, P. T. 1985b, November/December. What's it all about? *Change*. 32-36.

EWELL, P. T. 1987a. Establishing a campus-based assessment program: A framework for choice. *In*: Student outcomes assessment: A tool for improving teaching and learning. New directions for higher education, ed. D. F. Halpern. San Francisco: Jossey-Bass.

EWELL, P. T. 1987b, January/February. Assessment: Where are we? *Change*. 23-28.

FARMER, C. 1979. *Administrative evaluation*. 178-180. Richmond, VA: Higher Education Leadership and Management Society, Inc.

FIDLER, T. A. 1982. Advancing community college impact through business and industry. *In*: Institutional impacts on campus, community, and business constituencies. New directions for community colleges, ed. R. L. Alfred. 21-34. San Francisco: Jossey-Bass.

FIDLER, T. A. et al. 1978. *Mid-Ohio valley industrial needs assessment—1978*. Parkersburg, WV: Parkersburg Community College, Community Services Department.

FISKE, E. B. 1987, January 18. Colleges prodded to prove worth. *New York Times*. 1.

FITZGERALD, M. J., AND C. J. GRAFTON. 1981. Comparison and implications of peer and student evaluation for a community college faculty. *Community/Junior College Research Quarterly*. 5: 331-337.

FORD, M. 1979. New ideas: Will they work? *In*: Establishing effective programs. New directions for student services, eds. U. Delworth and G. R. Hanson. San Francisco: Jossey-Bass.

FORDYCE, J. W. 1972. Evaluation of student services in the community college. *In*: Student development programs in the community junior college, eds. T. O'Banion and A. Thurston. Englewood Cliffs, NJ: Prentice Hall.

GAPPA, J. M. 1984. *Part-time faculty: Higher education at a crossroads*. ASHE-ERIC Higher Education Research Report, Washington, DC: Association for the Study of Higher Education.

GARRISON, D. 1986, December/January. War without guns. *AACJC Journal*. 20-23.

GARRITY, R. J. 1984. Curricular excellence: The role of the advisory committee. *Community, Junior, and Technical College Journal*. 55: 40-41.

GILL, P. L., AND T.D. NOLAN. 1981. Program evaluation through follow-up—A faculty owned and operated model. *Community College Frontiers*. 9: 39-43.

GILMORE, G. M., KANE, M. T., AND NACCARATO, R. M. 1978. The generalizability of student ratings of instruction: Estimation of teacher and course components. *Journal of Educational Measurement*. 15: 1-13.

GLEASON, M. 1986, February. Getting a perspective on student evaluation. *AAHE Bulletin*. 10-13.

GOODRICH, T. J. 1978. Strategies for dealing with the issues of subjectivity in education. *Evaluation Quarterly*. 2: 631-645.

GOODWIN, H. I., AND E. R. SMITH. 1985. *Faculty and administrator evaluation: Constructing the instruments*. West Virginia University Press. 16-24.

GRASHA, A. 1977. *Assessing and developing faculty performance: Principles and models*. Cincinnati, OH: Communication and Education Associates.

GUBA, E., AND Y. LINCOLN. 1981. *Effective evaluation: Improving the usefulness of evaluation results through responsive and naturalistic approaches*. San Francisco: Jossey-Bass.

HAMMONS, J. 1987. Five potholes in the road to community college excellence. *Community College Review*. 15: 5-12.

HARPEL, R. L. 1976. Planning, budgeting, and evaluation in student affairs programs: A manual for administrators. *National Association of Student Personnel Journal*. 14: i-xx.

HARTMAN, J. 1986. Link up for gerontology. *Community, Junior, and Technical College Journal*. 56: 58-61.

HEEMANN, W. 1985. Criteria for evaluation: Advanced programs. Washington, DC: Council for the Advancement and Support of Education.

HENDRICKSON, R. M., AND B. A. LEE. 1983. *Academic employment and retrenchment: Judicial review and administrative action*. ASHE-ERIC Higher Education Research Report No. 8. Washington, DC: Association for the Study of Higher Education.

HERRSCHER, B. R. 1976. Instructional Effectiveness Inventory. Houston, TX: Center for Educational Development.

HOCHANADEL, G. 1986, October/November. Labette Community College. *AACJC Journal*. 68.

HODGKINSON, H. 1985. *All one system: Demographics of education, kindergarten through graduate school*. Washington, DC: Institute for Educational Leadership.

HOFSTADTER, R., AND W. METZGER. 1969. *The development of academic freedom in the United States*. New York: Columbia University Press.

HOLDSWORTH, R. 1984, November. No shrinking violet. *AACJC Journal*. 24-27.

HOYT, D. P. 1982. Using colleague ratings to evaluate the faculty member's contribution to instruction. *In*: Practices that improve teaching evaluation. New directions for teaching and learning, ed., French-Lazovik. 57-72. San Francisco: Jossey-Bass.

JACKSON, R. J. 1981. An analysis of corporate-community college relations. *Community Services Catalyst.* 11: 13-15.

KAPLAN, W. A. 1986. *The law of higher education.* San Francisco: Jossey-Bass.

KAUFFMAN, J. F. 1984. Assessing the quality of student services. *In*: Determining the effectiveness of campus services. New directions for institutional research, ed. R. A. Scott. San Francisco: Jossey-Bass.

KELLAMS, S. E., AND K. K. KYRE. 1978. Part-time faculty in four year colleges and universities. *In:* Employing part-time faculty. New directions for institutional research, ed. D. W. Leslie. San Francisco: Jossey-Bass.

KELLS, H. 1983. *Self-study processes: A guide for postsecondary institutions.* New York: American Council on Education/Macmillan.

KINNICK, M. K., AND O. T. LENNING. 1976. *The information needs of prospective students.* Resource paper prepared for the National Task Force for Better Information for Student Choice, National Center for Higher Education Management Systems, Boulder, CO.

KIRKWOOD, R. 1981. Process or outcomes—A false dichotomy. *In*: Quality—Higher education's principal challenge, ed. T. G. Stauffer. 63-68. Washington, DC: American Council on Education.

KOPECEK, R. J., AND S. K. KUBRIK. 1982. Opportunities for alumni relations. *In*: Advancing the two-year college. New directions for institutional advancement, eds. P.S. Bryant and J. A. Johnson. San Francisco: Jossey-Bass.

KUH, G. D., ed. 1979. *Evaluation in student affairs.* Cincinnati, OH: American College Personnel Association.

LAHTI, R. E. 1975. Improving performance appraisals. *Community and Junior College Journal.* 45: 8-10.

LARROWE, C. P. 1986. Reflections of a faculty grievance officer. *Academe.* 72: 16-19.

League for Innovation in Community Colleges. 1985. *A review of faculty evaluation systems at League for Innovation Colleges.* Laguna Hills, CA: Author.

LENNING, O. T. 1977. Assessing student progress in academic achievement. *In*: L. L. Baird (ed.), *Assessing student achievement and social progress.* San Francisco: Jossey-Bass.

LENNING, O. T., AND E. M. COOPER. 1978. *Guidebook for colleges and universities: Presenting information to prospective students.* Boulder, CO: The National Center for Higher Education Management Systems.

LESLIE, D. W. 1984, October. Part-time faculty: Legal and collective bargaining issues. *AAHE Bulletin.* 8-12.

LESLIE, D. W., KELLAMS, S. E., AND GUNNE, G. M. 1982. *Part-time faculty in American higher education*. New York: Praeger.

LESLIE, D. W., AND R. P. SATRYB. 1977. Writing grievance procedures on the basis of principle. *In*: Handbook of faculty bargaining, eds. G. Angell and E. Kelly. San Francisco: Jossey-Bass.

LISTON, E. J., AND C. V. WARD. 1984, November. The greenhouse effect. *AACJC Journal*. 20-23.

MANNING, W. 1987, February/March. The truly deceptive aspect of the value-added philosophy . . . Point. *AACJC Journal*. 52.

MARCUS, L. R., LEONE, A. O., AND GOLDBERG, E. D. 1983. *The path to excellence: Quality assurance in higher education*. ASHE-ERIC Higher Education Research Report, Washington, DC: Association for the Study of Higher Education.

MARSH, H. W. 1980. The influence of student, course, and instructor characteristics in evaluations of university teaching. *American Educational Research Journal*. 17: 219-237.

MARTORANA, S. V., AND P. H. GARLAND. 1984, November. The two-edged sword. *AACJC Journal*. 16-19.

MC CLEOD, M., AND R. CARTER. 1986. The measure of quality in two-year colleges. *Community College Review*. 13: 14-20.

MC CORKLE, C. O., AND S. O. ARCHIBALD.1982. *Management and leadership in higher education*. San Francisco: Jossey-Bass, 171-180.

MC DANIEL, J. W., AND R. LOMBARDI. 1972. Organization and administration of student personnel work in the community college. *In*: Student development programs in the community junior college. eds. T. O'Banion and A. Thurston. Englewood Cliffs, NJ: Prentice-Hall.

MC FADDEN, D. N. 1975. *USHER redesign model*. Columbus, OH: Battelle Center for Improved Education.

MC TARNAGHAN, R. E. 1986, Fall. How to assess undergraduate education? One state's perspective. *State Education Leader*. 3-4.

MILLER, R. I. 1974. *Developing programs for faculty evaluation*. San Francisco: Jossey-Bass.

MILLER, R. I. 1979. *The assessment of college performance*. San Francisco: Jossey-Bass.

MILLER, R. I. 1986. A ten year perspective on faculty evaluation. *International Journal of Institutional Management in Higher Education*. 10: 162-167.

MILLER, R. I. 1987. *Evaluating faculty for promotion and tenure*. San Francisco: Jossey-Bass.

MILLETT, J. D. 1980. *Management governance and leadership*. New York: AMACOM. 138-139.

MILTON, O., POLLIO, H. R., AND EISON, J. A. 1986. *Making sense of college grades*. San Francisco: Jossey-Bass.

MITZEL, H., ed. 1982. *The encyclopedia of educational research*. Fifth edition. New York: Free Press, 592-611.

MODEN, G. O., AND A. M. WILLIFORD. 1987, May. *A multi-dimensional approach to student outcomes assessment*. Paper presented at the 27th Annual Forum of the Association for Institutional Research, Kansas City, MO.

MOOMAW, W. E. 1977. Practices and problems in evaluating instruction. *In*: Renewing and evaluating teaching. New directions for higher education, ed. J.A. Centra. 77-91. San Francisco: Jossey-Bass.

MOON, R., ed. 1981. *New directions for a learning society*. New York: College Entrance Examination Board.

MORTIMER, K. P., ed. 1984. *Involvement in learning: Realizing the potential of American higher education*. Washington, DC: National Institute of Education.

NAISBITT, J. 1982. *Megatrends: Ten new directions transforming our lives*. New York: Warner Books.

National Institute of Education. 1984. *Involvement in learning: Realizing the potential of American higher education*. Washington, DC: the institute.

NICKENS, J. 1985, October/November. Is statewide exit testing for community college students a sound idea? Counterpoint. *AACJC Journal*. 53.

NOEL, L., AND D. SALURI. 1983. Setting and assessing outcomes: A fresh approach. *In*: A new look at successful programs, ed. J. E. Roueche. San Francisco: Jossey-Bass.

ORDOVENSKY, P. 1987, February 2. Special tests give students an edge. *USA Today*. 1-2.

OSTERKAMP, D., AND P. HULLETT. 1983. *Re-entry women and part-time students: An overview with relevant statistics*. Bakersfield, CA: Bakersfield College.

PACE, C. R. 1984, Fall. Historical perspectives on student outcomes: Assessment with implications for the future. *NASPA Journal*. 22: 10-18.

PALMER, J. 1983. How is quality measured at the community college? *Community College Review*. 11: 52-62.

PALMER, J. 1986. Sources and information: The social role of the community colleges. *In*: Active trusteeship for a changing era. New directions for community colleges, ed. C. F. Petty. 101-113. San Francisco: Jossey-Bass.

PALMER, S. E. 1987, May 6. Fearing loss of public confidence, some col-